AN ILLUSTRATED HISTORY OF THE
WEAPONS OF
WORLD WAR TWO

A comprehensive directory of the military weapons used in World War Two, from field artillery and tanks to torpedo boats and night fighters, with more than 180 photographs

Covers all the main weaponry of the Allies and the opposing military alliance, with specification boxes providing information on each technology • Donald Sommerville

This edition is published by Southwater,
an imprint of Anness Publishing Ltd,
Blaby Road, Wigston, Leicestershire LE18 4SE
Email: info@anness.com
Web: www.southwaterbooks.com; www.annesspublishing.com

Anness Publishing has a new picture agency outlet for images for
publishing, promotions or advertising. Please visit our website
www.practicalpictures.com for more information.

Publisher: Joanna Lorenz
Editorial Director: Helen Sudell
Editor: Elizabeth Young
Production Controller: Bessie Bai

Produced for Lorenz Books by Toucan Books:
Managing Director: Ellen Dupont
Editor: Marion Dent
Project Manager: Hannah Bowen
Designer: Elizabeth Healey
Cartographer: Julian Baker
Picture Researcher: Debra Weatherley
Indexer: Michael Dent

© Anness Publishing Ltd 2011

ETHICAL TRADING POLICY
At Anness Publishing we believe that business should be conducted
in an ethical and ecologically sustainable way, with respect for the
environment and a proper regard to the replacement of the natural
resources we employ.

As a publisher, we use a lot of wood pulp in high-quality paper
for printing, and that wood commonly comes from spruce trees.
We are therefore currently growing more than 750,000 trees in three
Scottish forest plantations: Berrymoss (130 hectares/320 acres),
West Touxhill (125 hectares/305 acres) and Deveron Forest
(75 hectares/185 acres). The forests we manage contain more than
3.5 times the number of trees employed each year in making
paper for the books we manufacture.

Because of this ongoing ecological investment programme, you,
as our customer, can have the pleasure and reassurance of knowing
that a tree is being cultivated on your behalf to naturally replace
the materials used to make the book you are holding.

Our forestry programme is run in accordance with the UK
Woodland Assurance Scheme (UKWAS) and will be certified
by the internationally recognized Forest Stewardship Council
(FSC). The FSC is a non-government organization dedicated to
promoting responsible management of the world's forests.
Certification ensures forests are managed in an environmentally
sustainable and socially responsible way. For further information
about this scheme, go to www.annesspublishing.com/trees

PICTURE CREDITS
akg-images 9t, 15t, 22b, 33b, 34t and b, 48b, /ullstein bild 9b, 10r, 11b,
12, 14b, 16b, 17t, 20br, 21t, 27b, 28t, 53b, 54t, 59tl, 64b, 66b, 81t,
Aviation-images.com 50r, 57tl, /H.Cowin 49l and r, 55t, 58r, 59r, 61t, 68b,
69m, /P. Jarrett 51b, 54b, 55b, 62b, 63b, 65tl, /Royal Aeronautical Society
62t, /TRHP 65tr, /Mark Wagner 57tr, /R. Winslade 65b, Cody Images
cover all, p1, p2, p3, p4 p5, CORBIS 13b, 28b, 34, 37l, 43t, 50l, 71b, 85bl,
89tr, 91tr, 92b, /Bettmann 69t, 79b, 8l, 84, 85br, 93b, /The Dmitri
Baltermants Collection 35tl, /Christel Gerstenberg 23b, /Hulton-
Deutsch Collection 41t and b, 43b, 67t, Getty Images /Hulton Archive
18bl, 19tr, 38r, 40b, 42b, 44t, 44br, 45b, 51t, 52b, 56bl, 56br, 58l, 60b, 64b,
66t, 70t, 71t, 91tl, /Time & Life Pictures 10bl, 26, 42t, 53t, 60t, 63t, 90,
95b, Photographs reproduced by permission of the Trustees of The
Imperial War Museum, London. 8r E 1416, 11t H 23836, 13t SE 358, 15r
B 15007, 15b H 36806, 18t BU 823, 20l BU 2756, 21tr B 15229, 22t TR
1800, 23t H 25860, 25tl TR 450, 25tr H 34424, 27t TR 1402, 29br H
37859, 33t BU 127, 35tr E 19296, 44bl MH 6810, 52t C 1653, 61b TR 37,
67b E (MOS) 1403, 68t CL 2946, 70b COL 353, 76b FL 14721, 77b A
28203, 78b A 24047, 80br A 30080, 83t A 2298, 86bl FL 1204, 87t C 4050,
88t A 2003, 93t A 21447, 94t A 9060, The Tank Museum (www.tankmu-
seum.org.uk) 16t, 17tr, 17b, 18br, 19tl, 21b, 29t and bl, 30l and r, 31l and
r, 32l and r, 33b, 38l, 39t and b, Topfoto.co.uk 95tr, /Alinari 85t,
/Artmedia/HIP 14t, /Feltz 48t, /Keystone 37r, /Roger Viollet 24r, US
Army Signal Corps (www.history.army.mil) 24l, US Naval Historical
Center 74l and r, 75r, 76t, 77t, 78t, 79t, 82t, 82b, 83b, 86r, 87b, 88b, 89tl
and b, 91b, 92t, 94b, 94tl.

Front cover main image shows: RAF Spitfire fighter aircraft of 41
Squadron, April 1944. Front cover clockwise from top left: Two
Soviet/Red Army 152mm ISU-152 self-propelled guns ford a river,
RAF munitions are stored for bombing raids on Germany; Wehrmacht
railway gun 21cm K12(E) firing, Germany; US Battleships of the New
Mexico class pictured at sea 1939. Front cover flap shows: RAF
Spitfire No. 453 at Ford airfield, England on D-day. Back cover
clockwise from top left shows: US Army Sherman M4 medium tank
fitted with RAF Spitfire No. 453 at Ford airfield, England on D-day;
US Soldier with "Bazooka"; Ground crew prepare to re-arm P-51
Mustang fighter with 0.50 calibre ammunition; Two Soviet/Red Army
152mm ISU-152 self-propelled guns ford a river; Wehrmacht railway
gun 21cm K12(E) firing; US Battleships of the New Mexico class
pictured at sea 1939; Junkers JU 87 Stuka dive bombers. Back cover
flap shows: RAF munitions are stored for bombing raids on Germany.
Spine shows: Russian IS-2 (Iosif Stalin) tanks, introduced in April
1944. These tanks are believed to be advancing through the ruins of a
German town. Page 1: US Army Sherman M4 medium tank fitted with
RAF Spitfire No. 453 at Ford airfield, England on D-day; page 2:
German battle-cruiser Scharnhorst; page 3 top: US Soldier with
"Bazooka"; page 3 bottom: Ground crew prepare to re-arm P-51
Mustang fighter with 0.50 calibre ammunition; page 4: Battle of
Midway, Japanese Mogami cl cruiser damaged; page 5 top: Australian
troops during the New Guinea Campaign on the 9 April 1942;
page 5 bottom: Junkers JU 87 Stuka dive bombers.

PUBLISHER'S NOTE
Although the advice and information in this book are believed to be
accurate and true at the time of going to press, neither the authors nor
the publisher can accept any legal responsibility or liability for any
errors or omissions that may be made.

Previously published as part of a larger volume, *The Complete Illustrated
History of World War II*

Contents

Introduction

Within a few years of its end many people even in the victorious countries were questioning if World War I had been a just and necessary war. This has never been true of World War II, either in the immediate aftermath or in longer historical retrospect. The unmitigated evil at the heart of Hitler's Germany and the unrestrained cruelty of the Japanese regime to its prisoners and subjects were both so plain that, at the time and since, few have argued that it was a war that was not worth fighting. Although the world soon moved into the Cold War, an era of potentially even more dangerous confrontation, few have ever suggested that the Allied lives lost in the war were lives sacrificed in vain.

Below: The japanese cruiser Mikuma on fire and sinking after being attacked by US dive-bombers during the Battle of Midway on the 6th of June, 1942.

Far more than any previous major war, WWII saw civilians effectively in the front line. In part this arose from the murderous nature of the totalitarian regimes of Hitler and Stalin, and the vicious racism of Japan's militarists, but the Anglo-American bombing campaigns meant that those countries' leaders also had far from clean hands.

Unlike World War I – the first war of the combat aircraft, the tank and the submarine – there were no new types of weapon of any importance introduced until almost the end of the war. The major military development was the extension of the use of air power to a level far beyond anything previously attempted or contemplated. Developments in radio and electronics also meant that, both in the air and on the ground, operations could be directed with a new level of sophistication – tank commanders could

Right: Australian troops during the New Guinea Campaign on the 9th April 1942. Troops are pictured at Port Moresby with a universal Carrier armed with the Vickers .303in (7.7mm) machine gun produced by Vickers Limited originally for the British Army.

Below right: The Luftwaffe Junkers JU 87 Stuka dive bombers was a German ground-attack aircraft. It was easily recognizable by its inverted gull wings, fixed spatted undercarriage, and its infamous wailing siren.

talk to each other; aircraft could be detected hundreds of miles away; and radar could find the periscope of a submerged submarine at sea.

The war's one new weapon was obviously the atom bomb, which clearly changed the nature of warfare for all time. Its level of destructive power was so great that even when no nuclear retaliation was possible, its owners might hesitate to use it. With such a dire threat to the future of humankind in existence, it was in a sense just as well that people had seen the flattened cityscape of Hiroshima and heard the dreadful evidence of the horrors of the Holocaust. The propagation of such knowledge of just how terrible wars can be may have served to make people and governments more likely to resolve their differences peacefully. This is perhaps the lasting benefit that World War II brought.

This expertly written work presents all the main weapons that were used during World War II. Divided into three chapters, Army Weapons, Air Force Weapons, and Naval Weapons, the key weapons used used by the Allied and opposing military forces are described. Listed chronologically, each weapon features information explaining how they worked, different types, the successes and failures, and the tactics that often decided the outcomes. All these elements combine to form a detailed history of the technologies and weapons of World War II and give an in-depth analysis on how the war was fought.

ARMY
WEAPONS

Tanks and infantry men are an important element of modern armies. Grenades, submachine-guns and rifles were the most common personal weapons for soldiers. This chapter examines all the main army weapons, from assault guns to special purpose armoured vehicles designed to clear obstacles and breach enemy defences.

Image: Russian IS-2 (Iosif Stalin) tanks, introduced in April 1944, advancing through the ruins of a German town.

Tanks, 1939–42

The successes of Germany's early-war campaigns were based on the power of the much-feared Panzer divisions, giving tanks a prominence in military affairs they had never before attained.

Tanks, as well as anti-tank weapons, were the only types of land-warfare weaponry that saw substantial development during WWII. In 1939 the most powerful tanks mainly had a gun in the 37mm (2pdr) class and were protected by up to 40mm (1.58in) armour. By 1942, 75mm (2.95in) weapons and twice as much armour were typical. These figures increased still further later in the war.

EARLY PANZERS

Nazi Germany's first tank, built during the mid-1930s, was the Panzerkampfwagen (PzKpfw) 1, a light two-man design armed only with machine-guns. This was soon joined by the slightly more powerful PzKpfw 2. Both saw combat into 1941. The best tanks in the Panzer divisions of 1939–41 were the next two in the series. The PzKpfw 3 was available in various marks in the early-war period. Up to April 1940 all carried a 3.7cm (1.46in) main gun but this was replaced by first a 42-calibre 5cm (1.97in) gun and then a more powerful 60-calibre 5cm. The PzKpfw 4 was originally conceived as an infantry-support vehicle and hence began life with a short (24-calibre) 7.5cm (2.95in) gun; by 1942 its 7.5cm gun was a version twice as long. For the first two or three years of the war the Germans also used many Czech-built tanks. The PzKpfw 38(*t*) was a powerful design of similar capabilities to the PzKpfw 3 of the time.

The British and French tanks facing this array in 1940 were a mixed bag; most were additionally

MATILDA 2

The Matilda was the only British tank to see combat throughout the war, remaining in use against the Japanese until 1945. Its main European service was in France and North Africa in 1940–1. (The example shown below is in Egypt, December 1940.) Its thick armour and reasonable anti-tank gun power made it a tough opponent then but it was very slow cross-country. Almost 3,000 were built.

WEIGHT: 26.9 tonnes
LENGTH: 5.6m (18ft 5in)
HEIGHT: 2.5m (8ft 3in)
ARMOUR: 78mm (3.1in)
ROAD SPEED: 25kph (15mph)
ARMAMENT: 1 x 2pdr (40mm) + 1 x machine-gun

Left: M3 Lee tanks and American troops in training in Northern Ireland in 1942. These were some of the first US soldiers to serve in Europe.

hampered by being dispersed in small infantry-support units. Various French designs like the Somua S-35 were well-armed and armoured but were made less efficient in action by their one-man turrets, in which the commander had to make tactical decisions and also load, aim and fire the gun.

Britain had a succession of light, medium and heavy tanks throughout the early-war years. The Light Tank Marks 5 and 6 were armed only with machine-guns – so they were useless for anti-tank combat – but did see extensive service in France and the early North African battles.

The medium (or cruiser) tanks went from the Mark 1, first produced in 1938, to the Mark 6 or Crusader, final versions of which appeared in 1942. All the cruiser tanks had reasonable armour and gun power, but they had appallingly unreliable engines and running gear.

The heavy tanks were better. The Matilda 2 carried the same 2pdr (40mm) gun as most of the cruisers and mounted 78mm (3.1in) armour, which made it very difficult indeed to knock out in its heyday of 1940–1. Its successors, the Valentine and Churchill, were robust and reliable, if under-gunned.

The USA's early-war tanks were the M3 Light Stuart and M3 Medium, known as the Lee in US service and the Grant in the slightly different form used by Britain. The Stuart, with a 37mm (1.46in) gun and 37mm armour, was fast and reliable. Updated as the M5, it was still used extensively in 1944–5. The Lee/Grant was an interim type, a hurried redesign of an earlier model to fit a 75mm

Above: An early-model Panzer 3 with 3.7cm (1.46in) gun during a river-crossing exercise in 1941.

(2.95in) gun, but only in a side sponson rather than a turret. Production ended in 1942.

SUPERIOR SOVIET TYPES

The most impressive Allied tanks were those of the Red Army. The early-war BT-7 was particularly fast and carried a reasonable 45mm (1.77in) gun, but the next generation of Russian tanks were the finest in service anywhere in their time. The heavy KV-1 came first, making its combat debut in the Russo-Finnish War in 1940. Its 76.2mm (3in) gun and 90mm (3.54in) armour outclassed anything the Germans had available in 1941. Even better was the medium T-34, sometimes described as the tank that won the war for the USSR. Fortunately for the Germans, comparatively few of these two designs were available in 1941.

SOMUA S-35

Designed in 1934–5 the Somua S-35 was intended as a fast "cavalry" tank and fulfilled this brief well. Some 300 saw combat during the 1940 Battle of France, including those shown below. The S-35 was well-armed and armoured but mechanically unreliable.

WEIGHT: 20 tonnes
LENGTH: 5.5m (18ft)
HEIGHT: 2.7m (8ft 10in)
HULL ARMOUR: 40mm (1.58in)
ROAD SPEED: 37kph (23mph)
ARMAMENT: 1 x 47mm (1.85in)
 + 1 x machine-gun

Anti-tank Guns, 1939–42

As tanks were steadily upgraded so, too, were the anti-tank guns used against them by the infantry and artillery. The first anti-tank guns were small, manoeuvrable and easy to conceal, but as they grew in size these qualities came under threat.

When tanks were initially introduced in WWI, the weapons used to counter them were either standard artillery guns or specially powerful rifles. Although anti-tank (AT) rifles were still used by most armies in 1939, it was clear in the 1930s that more powerful specialized AT weapons were needed by the infantry and other forces.

Germany's standard AT gun at the start of the war was a 3.7cm (1.46in) weapon made by the Rheinmetall company from 1936. This gun (formally the Panzerabwehrkanone [PaK] 36) was typical of those in service with other armies, too. It was mounted on a wheeled carriage, giving an overall weight of under half a tonne, and could readily be manhandled in action. It fired a 0.68kg (1.5lb) armour-piercing (AP) shot, cap-

Below: A Soviet 45mm (1.77in) M1937 anti-tank gun under fire.

able of defeating 31mm (1.22in) of armour angled at 30 degrees at a distance of 500m (550yd).

SOVIET AND US TYPES

The Soviet Model 1930 37mm gun had originally been developed by Rheinmetall and was very similar to the PaK 36. Japan also had a licence-built version of the PaK 36. The US Army M3A1 37mm, introduced in 1940, was slightly different, though examples of the German gun were studied by the American designers. Over 18,000 of these were produced. Although it was outclassed in Europe by late 1942, this gun saw most service in the Pacific against Japan's weaker tanks.

In 1939 Britain's standard weapon was the 2pdr (40mm), with similar performance, though on a rather heavier and more elaborate carriage. The Soviets also had the 45mm (1.77in) M1937, which was

slightly more powerful – and it was later replaced by a longer-barrelled M1942 version.

HEAVIER CALIBRES

By 1939 heavier weapons were being developed in the West. Germany stepped up to 5cm (1.97in) in the PaK 38, with more than double the armour penetration of the PaK 36.

3.7CM PAK 36

The 3.7cm PaK 36 anti-tank gun (shown below during a river-crossing operation in the Netherlands in 1940) was the German Army's standard weapon at the start of the war. It was replaced in most units by 1942. A similar weapon was mounted on the Panzer 3 and various other armoured vehicles.

CALIBRE: 3.7cm (1.46in) L/45
MUZZLE VELOCITY: 762m/sec (2,500ft/sec)
ARMOUR PENETRATION: 31mm (1.22in) at 30° at 500m (550yd)
WEIGHT OF SHOT: 0.68kg (1.5lb)

Britain's next type was the 6pdr (57mm), but this was slow to come into service because the switch in production from the 2pdr was delayed by the need to re-equip the army after Dunkirk. The USA's 57mm M1 was essentially a 6pdr manufactured under reverse Lend-Lease. There was also a Soviet 57mm M1943 weapon, produced in relatively limited numbers by Soviet standards. All these nations would make still bigger guns later in the war.

Germany was unusual in the early-war period in having both smaller- and larger-calibre

8.8CM FLAK 36

Throughout the war Allied tank crews feared the famous "eighty-eight" above all other German weapons. The example shown below is seen in service at El Alamein in 1942. The open spaces of the Desert War favoured the accuracy, armour penetration and range of this powerful gun.

CALIBRE: 8.8cm (3.46in) L/56
MUZZLE VELOCITY: 773m/sec
   (2,536ft/sec)
ARMOUR PENETRATION: 110mm
   (4.33in) at 500m (550yd)
   at 30° (99mm at 1,000m)
WEIGHT OF SHOT: 10.2kg (22.5lb)

weapons in regular AT use. The larger weapons were 8.8cm (3.46in) guns, originally produced for anti-aircraft (AA) service as the FlaK 18 and 36. As AA guns these already had the high muzzle velocity that was needed for the AT role and, unlike the AA weapons in most other armies, they were supplied with appropriate ammunition and specifically designated for such duty. These were by far the most formidable AT guns of the early-war period.

The smaller-calibre weapon was a so-called "squeeze-bore" design, in which the barrel tapered in size from breech to muzzle with a specially designed round being compressed as it passed down the barrel; the resulting build-up in pressure produced a very high muzzle velocity.

Above: British troops training with a 2pdr (40mm) anti-tank gun in 1942.

The only weapon of this type that saw significant service was Germany's sPzB 41, 2.8cm tapering to 2cm (1.1–0.79in). It had a similar AP performance to the PaK 36 and in the version for airborne troops weighed only 118kg (260lb). Its disadvantage was that it required tungsten-cored ammunition. Tungsten was very scarce in blockaded Germany, so production of these guns was ended in 1943.

This, however, was a pointer to future developments. Most early-war AT rounds were relatively simple solid-shot designs. From around 1942 capped designs and composite construction increasingly took over and would be extensively used in late-war weapons.

Field Artillery

Despite the more spectacular contributions of tanks and aircraft, World War II was a war dominated by artillery – more than half of all casualties on all battle fronts came from the ever more deadly concentrations of artillery fire.

The backbone of every army's firepower came from the medium-calibre guns of the field artillery units. Divisions invariably included an artillery component dedicated to the support of the division's units, usually on the basis of roughly one artillery battery (of perhaps six guns) for each infantry or tank battalion in the formation. Guns in the field artillery class were usually of 75–105mm (2.95–4.13in) calibre and fired shells, weighing 10–15kg (20–35lb), to a range of 12–15km (7.5–9.5 miles).

TYPES OF WEAPONS

A typical weapon of this type was the US Army's standard M2A1 105mm (4.13in) howitzer, a model that had been in service since 1934 and remained in use well into the Vietnam era. In common with most similar weapons, the M2A1 could fire a variety of different types of shell, including high explosive (HE), high explosive anti-tank (HEAT), white phosphorus, smoke, and even a leaflet-carrying type. A variety of propellant charges was also supplied for range adjustments.

Germany's standard weapons, the 10.5cm leFH 18 and slightly modified leFH 18/40, were essentially similar. Britain's main field gun – the 25pdr, with a calibre of 3.45in (87mm) – delivered a slightly smaller shell. However, it lost nothing in range and compensated by being very

Above: A German 10.5cm (4.13in) leFH 18 gun on the advance in the Ardennes in late 1944.

quick firing. Soviet divisional artillery weapons were a mix of smaller guns still (76.2mm/3in M1936, 1939 or 1942 guns and others) and heavier 122mm (4.8in) types (M1931 guns and M1938 howitzers and others). The 122mm howitzer had a similar range to the field guns discussed above and fired a 21.8kg (48lb) shell.

The other major Axis powers, Italy and Japan, had various 75mm (2.95in) and 105mm weapons, which were comparable in performance to the types noted above. However, neither nation used its artillery very effectively in action.

ORGANIZATION

Surprisingly, armies generally used fewer artillery weapons in WWII than in WWI. This was mainly because artillery tactics had changed and the techniques used for controlling artillery fire had advanced greatly.

Much of the artillery fire of WWI had been devoted to preparatory bombardments – programmes of shelling in advance of a battle designed to smash enemy positions and disrupt enemy forces. Germany and the Western Allies laid much less emphasis on this type of action in WWII, recognizing that it was of limited effectiveness and could often be counter-productive. Instead they emphasized neutralizing fire while an action was actually

Right: British artillerymen in Burma in action with a 3.7in (94mm) pack howitzer. Dating from WWI but with an improved mounting, the gun could fire a 9kg (20lb) shell.

occurring. The aim was to suppress enemy firepower and ability to manoeuvre.

Although the Red Army deployed a great mass of artillery its use tended to be less sophisticated, especially in the first couple of years of war. Battery commanders might well be the only personnel able to make the calculations needed for more complicated fire plans – their juniors might even be illiterate and have no watches for timing any switches of target.

Communications also played a vital part. Western artillery batteries routinely used forward observation officers (FOO), equipped with radios to direct and adjust their fire, and they had elaborate inter-connections between artillery units. An FOO could call for fire not only from his own battery but also, on occasion, from as many as several hundred other guns within a very short time. This process was assisted by the development of various standard patterns and timetables of fire that could very quickly be put in place by numerous artillery units. The superior British and American artillery organization established by 1943–5 was a significant factor in the Allied victory.

M3 105MM HOWITZER

The M3 105mm howitzer was a lighter version of the standard M2 field gun fitted with a shorter barrel. It was intended for use by airborne forces and was also employed by support companies of infantry units (as shown here in New Guinea in 1943–4). It had roughly two-thirds the range of the parent gun but fired similar ammunition. Some 2,500 were made.

CALIBRE: 105mm (4.13in)
WEIGHT: 1,135kg (2,500lb)
LENGTH: 3.94m (12ft 11in)
RANGE: 7,600m (8,300yd)
SHELL WEIGHT: 15kg (33lb) HE

Infantry Weapons

*At its most basic level, combat in land warfare depended on the qualities of the
infantry soldier's personal weapons. US Marines (like soldiers everywhere)
were taught: "My rifle is my best friend. … Without my rifle I am useless."*

The most common personal weapons for soldiers in all armies of World War II were hand grenades, submachine-guns and rifles.

Hand grenades were essential in every close-quarter engagement in all theatres of war and were used in vast numbers. Some grenades had offensive and defensive versions, the former relying solely on blast effects, the latter producing splinters or shrapnel in addition. Special-purpose grenades also included smoke and incendiary

Left: A German combat engineer clears a path through some barbed wire during an exercise. He is armed with a Stielhandgranate 24.

types. In outward appearance there were two main kinds: egg-shaped varieties like the British No. 36, based on the WWI Mills bomb, or stick designs like the German Stielhandgranate 24.

RIFLES

In 1939, as for decades before, the standard weapon for soldiers in all armies was a magazine-fed single-shot rifle, firing a bullet of roughly 7.7mm (0.3in) calibre. Such a round was lethal, and in theory could be fired accurately, to ranges well over 1,000m (1100yd), but it was an unlucky casualty indeed who was struck by a deliberately aimed shot at even a third of that distance.

The best such weapon was the USA's standard rifle, the 0.3in (7.62mm) M1 Garand, which had the advantage of being a semi-automatic design. Most other major rifles were of the older bolt-action type. The British 0.303in (7.7mm) Lee Enfield No. 4 was perhaps the best of these because its mechanism could be operated most speedily. However, other types like Germany's 7.92mm (0.312in) Mauser 98K, were also sturdy, accurate and reliable.

Left: An American recruit is instructed in marksmanship using an M1 Garand 0.3in (7.62mm) rifle.

Introduced in 1941, the Sten was cheap and quick to make. Over 4 million were produced in several slightly different marks. As well as being used by the British Army, it was sent to resistance forces who liked its simplicity and that it could use German ammunition.

SUBMACHINE-GUNS

Only during the final months of trench combat in WWI were submachine-guns used. They had the advantage over rifles of a far higher rate of fire (ammunition supply permitting), but they were difficult for even a well-trained soldier to fire accurately and also had short ranges because of the low-powered pistol rounds they employed.

The Red Army and the German Army made most widespread use of the submachinegun. The most common Soviet design (around 6 million made) was the 7.62mm PPSh-41. It was cheap but robust and its drum magazine held a very useful 71 rounds. Germany produced a series of weapons based on the 9mm (0.345in) MP38 and MP40 (which were erroneously referred to as the Schmeisser) that were effective and saw widespread service.

The principal design used by both the British and American armies in the early years of the war was the 0.45in (11.4mm) Thompson, more accurate and reliable than some, but heavy and expensive. Both Britain and

Above: Soviet infantry attacking. The man nearest the camera has a PPSh-41 submachine-gun. The men on the left have Mosin-Nagant M1891 7.62mm rifles, an old design with only a five-round magazine.

the USA also produced utility wartime designs: the 0.45in M3 "Grease Gun" for the USA and the 9mm Sten for Britain. British Stens were particularly inaccurate and of dubious reliability, but they were very cheap and easy to make – an important consideration when equipping a mass army from scratch after Dunkirk. Many were also sent to resistance groups.

ASSAULT RIFLES

In the later years of the war, the Germans introduced a number of self-loading assault rifles that included many of the virtues and avoided some of the vices of both the traditional rifle and the submachine-gun. The most important design was the Sturmgewehr 44, which used a new 7.92mm (0.312in) round that would be employed in the post-war years by early models of the AK-47 Kalashnikov.

SPECIFICATION: Sten Mark 2
CALIBRE: 9mm (0.354in)
LENGTH: 762mm (30in)
WEIGHT: 2.96kg (6lb 8oz)
BARREL LENGTH: 196mm (7.75in)
MUZZLE VELOCITY: 381m/sec (1,250ft/sec)
MAGAZINE: 32 rounds

In addition to the above, many combatants and non-combatant personnel in land, sea and air forces of all nations carried pistols (both revolvers and automatics) in a very wide variety of designs and calibres. These were used in action often enough as close-range weapons of last resort. However, they were seldom regarded as first-choice combat weapons.

Assault Guns

Tank turrets were expensive and difficult to build so heavily armoured vehicles, carrying powerful guns in simpler limited-traverse mountings, were also produced in numbers and used very effectively, notably on the Eastern Front.

Weapons in this category were almost exclusively the preserve of the German and Soviet armies. They had at least a reasonable degree of armour protection and carried weapons suitable both for anti-armour use and for direct fire support of assaulting troops and tanks. (Self-propelled guns in Anglo-American service are described in the self-propelled artillery and anti-tank gun categories – along with other Soviet and German designs – which better describe their capabilities and operational uses.)

Even with these limitations the number of vehicles that belong in this category is quite large. Soviet types include the SU-45, -57, -76, -85, -100, -122 and -152, and JSU-122 and -152 designs, too (the figures indicate the calibre of gun fitted). Germany fielded a similar variety. Accordingly, only a few examples on each side can be described.

SU-85

The SU-85 was designed to provide better anti-tank performance than the T-34/76. It was produced during 1943–4 but phased out when the T-34/85 entered service. The example shown is in German service after being captured.

WEIGHT: 29.4 tonnes
HULL LENGTH: 5.92m (19ft 5in)
HEIGHT: 2.54m (8ft 4in)
ARMAMENT: 85mm (3.35in)
   D-5 M1943
ARMOUR: 54mm (2.13in) max.
ROAD SPEED: 55kph (34mph)

FIRST DESIGNS

Germany's Sturmgeschütz 3, based on the Panzer 3 chassis, was the first notable weapon of this type. Versions of this design would serve throughout the war from 1940 and, indeed, become Germany's most-produced armoured fighting vehicle (AFV), with over 9,000 made.

Initially the StuG 3 was designed solely for infantry support with a short (L/24 – 24-calibre) 7.5cm (2.95in) gun mounted in the forward superstructure with limited traverse. Later models added first an L/43 7.5cm and then a more powerful L/48 gun to gain an effective anti-tank capability. There was also an essentially similar StuG 4 and a version fitting the 10.5cm (4.13in) howitzer. A further vehicle with comparable capabilities was the Hetzer, a design based on the PzKpfw 38(*t*) chassis and also carrying the L/48 7.5cm gun.

In a different category were various *Jagdpanzer* (usually translated as "tank destroyer") vehicles (confusingly, the Jagdpanzer 4 was really an updated StuG 4, rather than an entirely new type). Three vehicles of this sort should be mentioned.

First was the Elefant, or Ferdinand, based on an alternative design for the Tiger tank. It carried the most formidable

Left: A knocked-out Jagdpanther being examined by an American soldier in early 1945.

Above: A StuG 3 passes by a knocked-out T-34 during fighting in Poland in 1944.

SU-100

Like the SU-85, the SU-100 was based on the T-34 chassis, but with the more powerful 100mm D-10 gun. Full-scale production started in September 1944 and it saw significant service in 1945.

WEIGHT: 32.5 tonnes
HULL LENGTH: 5.92m (19ft 5in)
HEIGHT: 2.54m (8ft 4in)
ARMAMENT: 100mm (3.94in) D-10 M1944
ARMOUR: 75mm (2.95in) hull front
ROAD SPEED: 48kph (30mph)

version of the famous "eighty-eight", the PaK 43 L/71 8.8cm (3.46in) gun, behind very thick armour. Mechanically unreliable and lacking secondary armament to fend off infantry attack, it was not a success.

The Jagdpanther carried the same gun and was well armoured and agile; overall it was probably the most effective tank destroyer of the war. Its larger stablemate, the Jagdtiger, mounted a massive 12.8cm (5.04in) gun, the most powerful anti-tank gun of the war, behind armour up to 250mm (9.84in) thick, but was clumsy and unreliable. Most tellingly, for all their power, the total production of these types was roughly 90 Elefants, 390 Jagdpanthers and 80 Jagdtigers – never enough to stave off Germany's defeat.

SOVIET RESPONSES

The first significant Soviet design was the SU-76, which carried the M1942 76.2mm (3in) gun in an open-topped mount on a light-tank chassis. It was designed in response to the German StuG types; over 12,000 were

JAGDTIGER

The Jagdtiger first saw service in late 1944 and a few fought in the Battle of the Bulge. The basic vehicle was a variant of the Tiger 2 chassis, but it was under-powered and hence prone to breakdowns. Only two battalions using Jagdtigers were formed.

WEIGHT: 70 tonnes
HULL LENGTH: 7.39m (24ft 3in)
HEIGHT: 2.95m (9ft 8in)
ARMAMENT: 12.8cm (5.04in) PaK 44 + 1 x machine-gun
ARMOUR: 250mm (9.84in) max.
ROAD SPEED: 38kph (24mph)

built. Substantially more powerful were the SU-85 introduced in 1943 and SU-100 of late 1944. Neither of these had the same scale of armour as the German tank destroyers, but the SU-100 in particular had the gun power to deal with most German AFVs. By way of comparison at least 1,500 SU-100s were built by mid-1945.

The heaviest Soviet assault-gun types carried 122mm (4.8in) and 152mm (5.98in) guns. These weapons were not primarily designed for anti-tank use, but their heavy shells meant that they had significant anti-tank capabilities nonetheless and were often used in this role.

Light Armoured Vehicles

With the increasing mechanization of warfare generally, it was natural that the scouting and other support roles were filled by armoured vehicles. Armoured cars and personnel carriers accordingly proliferated in all armies in the European war.

Every army in World War II used armoured vehicles in scouting and support roles. Dozens of types were produced and most of these had numerous substantially different variants, so naturally only a selection can be discussed here.

BRITISH AND US TYPES

It is appropriate to begin with the most-produced armoured vehicle ever, the British Army's Bren, or Universal Carrier, of which over 100,000 were made. It could carry a machine-gun or mortar and its ammunition into action, tow a light anti-tank gun or serve in the scouting role, among many other tasks.

Britain was also a substantial user of wheeled armoured cars and their unarmed cousins – the scout cars. The most-produced types were the Daimler Dingo and Humber scout cars. Over 6,000 of the two-man Dingo were made. It had 30mm (1.2in) armour and such refinements as

Above: A British Humber armoured car in northern France in 1944.

run-flat tyres and transmission with five forward and reverse gears. Humber and Daimler (in that order) made the most common armoured cars too, both types being in use from 1941. Heavy armoured cars included the indigenous AEC design and the American-built T17 Staghound. Britain also relied on the USA for various (usually half-tracked) personnel carriers and similar vehicles.

Unlike Britain, the USA built and used relatively few armoured car types. By far the most important was the M8, known as the Greyhound in British service. This carried a 37mm (1.46in) gun and had

Left: An American M8 armoured car during training for D-Day "somewhere in England" in 1944.

originally been conceived for the tank-destroyer role. The most important American scout car was the White M3, with over 20,000 built. This could carry up to seven men plus the driver.

The US and German Armies made extensive use of half-tracked vehicles. These had much of the cross-country performance of fully-tracked vehicles but were easier and cheaper to build because of their

SDKFZ 251

Initially designed to carry the infantry in armoured divisions, the SdKfz 251 appeared in over 20 variants for other roles, including anti-aircraft, anti-tank and command vehicles. About 13,500 were built in all.

WEIGHT: 7.9 tonnes
LENGTH: 5.8m (19ft)
HEIGHT: 1.75m (5ft 9in)
WIDTH: 2.1m (6ft 11in)
ROAD SPEED: 53kph (33mph)
ENGINE: 120bhp Maybach HL42
ARMOUR: 15mm (0.6in) max.

Above: An M3 half track leads a US column in Germany, 1945.

simpler wheeled steering. US models included the smaller M2 and M9, and the larger M3 and M5. The M3 and M5 were 9-tonne vehicles that could carry a full infantry squad. All four were widely used in general front-line transport roles. In addition there were many variants carrying anti-aircraft, anti-tank and close-support weapons. Many US half tracks and scout cars were supplied to the Soviets.

GERMAN DESIGNS

The smallest and most unusual vehicle in Germany's half-track class was the SdKfz 2 Kettenkrad, in effect a half-track cargo motorcycle, of which over 8,000 were made. More important were the more conventional 5.9-tonne SdKfz 250 and its derivatives, as well as the larger 7.9-tonne SdKfz 251 and its numerous variants. These types were a little less mobile than the

US M2/M3, in part because the front wheels were unpowered, but they served in a similar variety of personnel, transport and weapon-carrying roles. Many were used as command vehicles, being fitted in the early-war years with large and conspicuous "bedstead" aerials for the radios they carried.

Germany also had a variety of 4-, 6- and 8-wheeled armoured cars. The 4-wheel SdKfz 221 was a 4-tonne vehicle with two crew and armed with a single machine-gun. The 6-wheel types were pre-war designs and were mostly withdrawn from service by 1941 or so. They were superseded by the 8 x 8 types from 1937.

The 8-wheel SdKfz 232 carried a 2cm (0.79in) cannon and a machine-gun (confusingly, there was also a 6-wheel SdKfz 232 and other overlapping designa-

Right: The British AEC Mark 3 heavy armoured car carried a 75mm (2.95in) gun.

BREN GUN CARRIER

The Universal Carrier (as the standardized examples were known from 1940) was the principal British utility vehicle. It often carried light weapons like the Boys anti-tank rifle and Bren Gun, seen here.

SPECIFICATION: Universal Carrier
WEIGHT: 4.3 tonnes
LENGTH: 3.75m (12ft 4in)
HEIGHT: 1.6m (5ft 3in)
WIDTH: 2.1m (6ft 11in)
ROAD SPEED: 32kph (20mph)
ENGINE: 85bhp Ford V8
ARMOUR: 10mm (0.4in) max.

tions). It was an 8.8-tonne vehicle with a crew of four, including a second driver in the rear of the fighting compartment who could drive the vehicle in reverse. The heaviest variant was the SdKfz 234 Puma, with a 7.5cm (2.95in) anti-tank gun.

Medium Tanks, 1942–5

Although their activities were increasingly constrained by air, artillery and infantry weapons, tanks still played a decisive role in combat, especially the intermediate-sized designs that appeared by the thousand on most European battlefields.

As tanks developed, competition between increased gun power and thicker armour naturally continued, but even more important was sheer quantity.

MASS PRODUCTION

Although Germany's PzKpfw 5 Panther was the most formidable tank discussed here, only some 6,000 were built compared to over 40,000 Soviet T-34s and 50,000 American Shermans. (There is no exact definition of the difference between a medium and a heavy tank but included here are tanks, regardless of weight, that normally served in the armoured regiments of standard armoured divisions, rather than in separate heavy tank units.)

The T-34 had set the benchmark for future designs during its first significant combats in 1941. It continued to give effective service in only slightly modified forms into 1944. By then its 76.2mm (3in) gun was insufficient to tackle the latest German types. From early 1944 a much better version – the T-34/85, carrying an 85mm (3.35in) gun – was produced. As well as sufficient gun power to destroy a Panther at normal battle ranges, this had a three-man turret. Previously the T-34 commander was also the gunner but now he could concentrate on his main role, which greatly improved combat efficiency.

The principal Anglo-American tank of the later-war years was the American M4 Sherman. When it appeared in 1942 this was broadly comparable with the contemporary T-34/76 or the later versions of the PzKpfw 4 (which would continue in service to the end of the war). Its 75mm (2.95in) main gun then had adequate power and it matched reasonable armour with excellent manoeuvrability and reliability. It was judged to be of sufficient quality that for a time US authorities halted development work on a successor to concentrate on mass production of this design (in many minor variants). Unfortunately this proved to be

Below: A cast-hull, 75mm-armed model of a Sherman in Italy in 1944.

COMET A34

The Comet A34 was the final vehicle in the British series of cruiser tanks in service throughout the war. It was a development of the Cromwell, with a much better gun based on the 17pdr and stronger, more reliable suspension.

WEIGHT: 33.2 tonnes
ARMAMENT: 1 x 77mm (3in) gun, 2 x machine-guns
ARMOUR: 101mm (4in) max.
CREW: 5
ROAD SPEED: 50kph (31mph)

Above: A Panther in action on the Eastern Front. Far too few Panthers were built to cope with the flood of Allied Shermans and T-34s.

T-34/85

Some 22,500 T-34/85 tanks were built in 1944–5. As well as having a better gun and improved internal arrangements, it retained the wide tracks and good cross-country performance of the earlier T-34/76 models.

WEIGHT: 32 tonnes
ARMAMENT: 1 x 85mm (3.35in) ZiS S53 gun, 2 x machine-guns
ARMOUR: 90mm (3.5in)
CREW: 5
ROAD SPEED: 50kph (31mph)

an unwise decision as, by 1944–5, its weaknesses had become very plain. The 75mm gun could not penetrate the frontal armour of a Panther or Tiger at all, and when hit itself the Sherman usually quickly burst into flames – a nightmare situation for any tank crewman.

BETTER SHERMANS

Improved versions did come into service by 1944–5. Some US Shermans were fitted with a more powerful 76mm (3in) gun and had better ammunition stowage, which reduced the fire problem. But the only model with truly adequate firepower was Britain's Sherman Firefly, with a version of the 17pdr (76mm) anti-tank gun. Even this had drawbacks: rate of fire was slow and Fireflies were often singled out as priority targets by German tanks.

Britain also had indigenous designs, developed from the early-war cruiser tank series. The Cromwell, in widespread use in 1944, was very fast and, unlike its predecessors, fairly reliable. However, it carried the same 75mm gun as the Sherman and had similar armour thickness. It was developed into the

SHERMAN FIREFLY

The Firefly was a conversion, not a new-build design. The most important change was the larger turret to fit the more powerful gun, but the hull machine-gun and radio operator were also omitted and the space used for ammunition.

WEIGHT: 32.5 tonnes
ARMAMENT: 1 x 17pdr (76mm) gun, 1 x machine-gun
ARMOUR: 76mm (3in)
CREW: 4
ROAD SPEED: 39kph (24mph)

Comet, in service from the autumn of 1944, with similar virtues and a version of the 17pdr gun, making it the first wholly British tank of the war with adequate firepower.

By 1944–5 the state of the art was defined by the Panther. Judged by its weight (45 tonnes) this was a heavy tank. It might be more accurately described by the post-war description "main battle tank" for its mix of thick armour, reasonable speed and, above all, substantial gun power. Its gun was an extremely potent 7.5cm KwK 42 and it had very thick and well-sloped armour. Mobility and reliability were its weaknesses, but it was a formidable opponent.

Infantry Support Weapons

Although all infantrymen carried personal weapons, success in battle often came from their heavier equipment. Infantry firepower from the fire-team to battalion level depended above all on machine-guns and mortars.

The principal support weapons employed within infantry units were machine-guns and mortars. Both categories included lighter weapons designed to be manoeuvred quickly between locations, and heavier types for use from longer-established positions in both defence and attack.

LIGHT MACHINE-GUNS

Infantry units in all armies worked in squads of roughly ten men with one or more light machine-guns providing the squad's main firepower in both attack and defence. Weapons of this type included the Soviet 7.62mm (0.3in) Degtyarev DP1928, the British 0.303in (7.7mm) Bren and the US 0.3in (7.62mm) Browning Automatic Rifle (BAR), all of them normally

bipod-mounted and magazine-fed. The Bren, highly accurate and reliable, and the Degtyarev, with a very useful 47-round magazine, were both more successful designs than the BAR, which was clumsy in action and had a smaller 20-round

Above: A British Bren gunner firing on German positions at Monte Cassino in Italy in early 1944.

magazine. Minor weapons also included France's 7.5mm (0.295in) Châtellerault.

HEAVY MACHINE-GUNS

Most armies had battalion or regimental support companies equipped with machine-guns for use in the sustained-fire role, aiming to deny areas of ground to the enemy in either attack or defence. These weapons were usually tripod-mounted and physically heavier than the squad light machine-guns, but not necessarily in larger calibres.

In fact the German Army used its MG34 and MG42 both as bipod manoeuvre weapons and on tripod mountings in

Left: A German MG34 on a tripod mount for use as a heavy machine-gun on the Eastern Front in 1941.

3-INCH MORTAR

Britain's 3-inch mortar was used throughout the war by the support companies of British infantry battalions. Versions were produced with varying barrel lengths – 130cm (51in) was standard. A lighter 76cm (30in) barrel, designed for jungle warfare, proved to be rather inaccurate.

CALIBRE: 76.2mm (3in)
WEIGHT: 57.2kg (126lb) – barrel 20kg (44lb), base plate 16.8kg (37lb), bipod 20.4kg (45lb)
RANGE: 2,560m (2,800yd)
BOMB WEIGHT: 4.5kg (10lb)

the sustained-fire role. The US Army filled this latter requirement with the 0.3in Browning M1917 (also used as a light machine-gun); Britain had the 0.303in Vickers; and the Soviets employed the 7.62mm PM1910 and Goryunov SG43. All were belt-fed and thoroughly reliable, though the PM1910 was particularly heavy.

Other nations' designs were often less satisfactory. The Italian Breda 6.5mm (0.256in) Modello 1930 light machine-gun and the heavier Fiat-Revelli Modello 1935 (in the same calibre) were both very prone to jamming.

Various armies also had heavy-calibre machine-guns, often used in a combination of ground and anti-aircraft roles and also commonly fitted to armoured vehicles. Notable types were the Soviet 12.7mm (0.5in) DShK1938 and the American 0.5in Browning M2 HB.

MORTARS

Infantry mortars came in two main calibres: roughly 50mm (2in) and 80mm (3in). Japan's 50mm (1.97in) Type 89 was typical of the smaller weapons, firing a 0.8kg (1.76lb) bomb up to 650m (700yd). Allied troops called it the "Knee Mortar", erroneously thinking it could be fired safely while balanced on a soldier's leg.

Another simple design was Britain's 2-inch mortar, which could fire a 1.1kg (2.4lb) bomb some 500m (550yd). In the larger calibres, several countries used versions of a French Brandt design, which included the American 81mm (3.19in) M1, firing a 4.8kg (10.6lb) bomb 2,250m (2,450yd). The Soviet 82mm (3.23in) PM37 and the Japanese 81mm Type 99 had a similar performance. Most mortars in this class came in three man-portable (but still very heavy) parts: barrel, base plate, bipod.

FLAMETHROWERS

Every major army used man-portable flamethrowers for such specialist tasks as bunker-busting. All had similar capabilities and similar drawbacks. All were very heavy (up to 40kg/90lb), and had a limited range (40–50m/yd) and a modest fuel supply (10 seconds or less).

Operating them was hazardous in the extreme, not least because flamethrower men could expect no mercy if they were captured by an enemy. Probably the most prolific use of flamethrowers was by the US Marine Corps in the battles for the Pacific islands.

Below: A German soldier with a Flammenwerfer 35, a particularly heavy early-war flamethrower design.

Anti-aircraft Guns

Although a single rifle bullet could bring down an aircraft, effective anti-aircraft fire usually depended on a combination of automatic weapons and slower-firing medium guns with greater destructive power and range.

In the course of WWII many thousands of aircraft on all sides were brought down by fire from the ground. High-flying heavy bombers or long-range fighters and low-altitude ground-attack aircraft were all vulnerable, though usually to different weapons. As in most other classes of land-warfare weapons, the types of anti-aircraft (AA) guns in service changed little during 1939–45, though ammunition and control equipment developed substantially.

LIGHT AA GUNS

Since lower-flying aircraft appear to be travelling faster to an observer on the ground, weapons to shoot down such planes have to be capable of traversing quickly and firing multiple shots rapidly, since a target might only be in sight for a few moments. In practice this meant weapons of roughly 40mm (1.5in) or less, typically firing a shell weighing less than 1kg (2.2lb) to an effective ceiling of up to 3,500m (11,500ft).

Although soldiers could and did attempt to engage aircraft with firearms of every kind up to and including standard machine-guns on specially adapted mounts, the smallest purpose-built AA system in widespread use with a major army was the American "Quad Fifty". This was a quadruple mounting carrying four 0.5in (12.7mm) M2 Browning heavy machine-guns, which appeared both on a towed trailer and on various self-propelled mounts. However, this was never entirely satisfactory as the individual rounds lacked sufficient striking power to bring down an enemy aircraft reliably.

The Germans had a 2cm (0.79in) weapon (and also developed a four-gun mount) but this had similar shortcomings. Japan, Italy and Britain had similar single-barrel 20mm weapons. Some of the British and Japanese weapons were based on a design originating with the Swiss Oerlikon company.

The next step up for Germany and the USA was to 3.7cm (1.46in), a calibre also used by the Soviets. Britain's main light AA gun was the 40mm (1.58in), built under licence from the Swedish Bofors company, a weapon also used by many other combatant nations. This fired a 0.9kg (2lb) high-explosive shell at a practical rate of 80–100rds/min.

Like most guns in this class the Bofors was usually fitted with simple visual sights, which were often the only ones used. Like other guns it also had various

---

M3 3-INCH GUN

The M3 3-inch gun was the standard US medium anti-aircraft gun in the early part of the war but was gradually replaced by the M3 90mm. Both guns were also used in ground roles, like this 3-inch shown in New Guinea in 1943.

CALIBRE: 3in (76.2mm)
SHELL WEIGHT: 5.6kg (12.3lb)
RATE OF FIRE: 25rds/min
EFFECTIVE CEILING: 9,100m (30,000ft)
MUZZLE VELOCITY: 853m/sec (2,800ft/sec) – HE shell

Right: A German Flakvierling quad 2cm (0.79in) Flak 38, in northern France in 1944.

Above: A British 3.7in (94mm) gun in action at night. Like many other British AA batteries, this one had a mixed male and female complement.

mechanical predictor sights (the type depending on the country), designed to help the gunners allow sufficient "lead" ahead of a fast-moving target.

HEAVY AA GUNS

Small numbers of guns of around 127mm (5in) were used by various nations, including the German 12.8cm (5.04in) FlaK 40, the US 120mm (4.72in) M1 and Britain's 5.25in (135mm). However, these were at the point where the gain in ceiling and striking power from the larger calibre began to be outweighed by slow rate of fire and clumsiness in action.

More common were lighter weapons similar to Germany's "Eighty-eight", various versions of an 8.8cm (3.46in) gun firing a 9.4kg (20.7lb) shell to over 8,000m (26,200ft). Britain's 3.7in (94mm) and the US 90mm (3.54in) weapons were broadly comparable. Like the Eighty-eight the 90mm on the M2 mount could be used as an anti-tank weapon.

HITTING THE TARGET

In the early-war years all AA guns had to rely, at best, on mechanical predictors calculating where to aim by using human estimates of aircraft height, speed and course.

During the war these were gradually replaced by radar systems which, among other advantages, could be used suc-

cessfully at night or through cloud. Heavier AA shells initially relied on time or barometric fuses which, when set using radar information, could indeed be extremely accurate.

Better still was an Anglo-American development, the proximity fuse, in effect a radar set that could be fitted in a shell to detonate it when it went close to a target. This was used with great success later in the war against Japanese kamikazes and German V-1 missiles.

Heavy Artillery

The big guns of the heavy artillery were among the most fearsome land warfare weapons of WWII. They also appeared by the hundred, or more – the Soviets used over 16,000 guns of all calibres in their final attack on Berlin in 1945.

Josef Stalin is said to have described artillery as the "god of war". No soldier on the receiving end of a bombardment from the heavy guns of any major army would have been likely to disagree. Heavy artillery weapons were usually allocated to higher formations (corps and armies or similar) and would be capable of switching their support from unit to unit, both in defence and in attack.

ARTILLERY TACTICS

As in other categories of artillery weapon, the Soviets were the most prolific users of heavy guns. Britain and the USA had the most sophisticated organization, able to shoot elaborate suppressive bombardment plans and to respond rapidly to events with stunning concentrations of firepower.

There were numerous weapons of this class in use: Germany had over 200 types of artillery weapon (of all calibres) in service. To give a more particular example, the Soviets had at least five models of 152mm (5.98in) howitzer and two 152mm guns. Accordingly only a representative sample can be discussed here.

Most armies had weapons closely comparable to the Soviet designs just mentioned, firing a shell of roughly 45kg (100lb) to a range of 15km (9.3 miles) for higher-trajectory howitzers or up to 27km (17 miles) for flatter-trajectory guns. Along with their different firing characteristics, the howitzers were also lighter overall and, therefore, usually more mobile and normally cheaper and easier to build, by no means a trivial consideration.

Britain's 5.5in (140mm) gun was typical. It fired a standard 45.4kg (100lb) shell to 14.8km (9.2 miles), or a 37kg (82lb) shell to 16.6km (10.3 miles). A little over 6 tonnes in action, it had a maximum rate of fire of perhaps 3 rounds a minute. The USA's 155mm (6.1in) Gun M1 fired a slightly lighter shell to a range of over 23km (14.3 miles), but the gun and mounting were twice as heavy overall as the 5.5in. Lesser-known but also effective types included Italy's 149mm (5.87in) Cannone da 149/40 M35 and France's 155mm M1932 Schneider.

SUPER-HEAVY WEAPONS

Most nations also included heavier guns and howitzers in their armoury. The US 8in (203mm) Gun M1 came into service mid-war. It could fire a 109kg (240lb) shell 35.5km (22 miles) on long-range-bombardment and counter-battery missions. Bigger still was its contemporary the 240mm (9.45in) Howitzer M1 with a 157kg (346lb) shell and a range of 23km (14.3 miles).

Left: A US 155mm (6.1in) M1 "Long Tom" gun, in action on Leyte during November 1944. The split-trail design gave a very stable firing platform.

5.5-INCH GUN

The British 5.5in (140mm) gun was introduced in 1940 and saw widespread service (the example shown is in Italy in 1943). There was also a slightly longer-ranged 4.5in (114mm) weapon mounted on the same carriage.

CALIBRE: 5.5in (140mm)
WEIGHT IN ACTION: 6.3 tonnes
SHELL WEIGHT: 45.4kg (100lb)
   or 37kg (82lb)
RANGE: 14.8km (16,200yd) –
   100lb shell; 16.5km
   (18,100yd) – 82lb shell
MUZZLE VELOCITY: 619m/sec
   (2,030ft/sec) max.
CREW: 10
RATE OF FIRE: 3rds/min
   max.

Railway guns were a particular German speciality including the longest-range and heaviest-calibre weapons to see action during the war.

The best-known of these was the 28cm (11in) K5 (E), employed against the Allied beachhead at Anzio among other places. This fired a 255kg (562lb) shell 63km (39 miles) or up to 86.5km (54 miles) with rocket assistance. A 28cm gun was reworked to 31cm (12.2in) calibre for test-firing a fine-stabilized round an even more astonishing 150km (93 miles).

The biggest weapon of all was a massive 80cm (31.5in) calibre. Two such guns were built, but only one is known to have been used (in the German siege of Sevastopol in 1942). The gun weighed some 1,350 tonnes in action, moved on two sets of railway tracks and fired a 7-tonne high-explosive shell up to 47km (29 miles). The design and industrial effort required to produce such a weapon was wholly disproportionate to its highly limited combat worth.

Below: A battery of German 15cm (5.91in) Kanone (E) railway guns in position near the French border in 1940. In fact few of these weapons saw action.

Special Purpose Armoured Vehicles

Clearing obstacles and breaching enemy defences were traditionally the tasks of army engineers. Modified tanks and other vehicles designed to carry out these roles were an important factor on D-Day and in other battles.

Battles to overcome elaborate enemy defences as part of an ongoing land campaign, and during waterborne landings at the start of one, were a recurring feature of the Allied counter-offensives in the second half of WWII. Clearing mines, crossing ditches and rivers, as well as destroying enemy strong points were among the tasks required. In line with the mechanization of many aspects of warfare, specialized armoured vehicles to undertake these duties saw significant service – most famously the "Funnies" of the British 79th Armoured Division, which saw action during the D-Day landings and thereafter.

MINE CLEARING

Two main mine-clearing tank types were developed: flails and rollers. Flails carried a rotating drum fitted with chains on the front that beat the ground as the tank drove forward, exploding

Below: DD Sherman tanks during a training exercise. The second tank has not yet lowered its flotation screen, but others have and are immediately ready to fight.

Above: A German Bergepanzer 3 armoured recovery vehicle assists a broken-down Panther battle tank.

mines in its path. These were first used in Matilda Scorpion form at the Battle of El Alamein in October 1942 and, later in the war, appeared in improved Sherman Crab versions. The US Army developed T1 mine rollers that featured an arrangement of steel discs pushed ahead of the tank.

OBSTACLE CROSSING

Ditches and walls were also often encountered. Some tanks were equipped to carry fascines

or similar material, which could be dropped into the gap or provide a ramp. Other tanks, notably the Churchill ARK, simply drove into the ditches or up to the walls themselves and then extended ramps in front and behind, so that subsequent vehicles could just drive over the top. The Carpet or Bobbin tanks unrolled a drum of matting over sandy beaches or similar difficult ground – and this provided a roadway for following wheeled vehicles.

All the major armies of the European war also had various forms of bridge-laying equipment. Germany deployed a

Above: A US T1 Mine Exploder in France in 1944. The 18-tonne rollers could be pushed in front of the Sherman tank at 8kph (5mph).

Above: A Churchill AVRE in late 1944, showing its spigot mortar and obstacle-crossing fascine.

small number of Bruckenleger 4 vehicles, derived from the Panzer 4, in France in 1940, but they were little used. Britain and the USA had Churchill and Sherman bridge-layers.

Perhaps the most important vehicle in this class was the British Churchill Armoured Vehicle Royal Engineers (AVRE). This could carry and position fascines or a short bridge and in addition mounted a spigot mortar to fire demolition charges at pillboxes or other enemy positions. Over 500 AVREs were built; they were extensively used in 1944–5.

NORMANDY BATTLES
One adaptation relatively seldom used, other than on D-Day, was also significant. These were the so-called Duplex Drive (DD) tanks – ordinary battle tanks that were made amphibious by being fitted with canvas screens to raise around the hull

Right: A Churchill Carpet during training for D-Day. The Carpet's matting could help wheeled vehicles cross barbed-wire obstacles.

and a propeller to drive them through the water at some 7kph (4mph). As soon as they reached the landing beach, the tanks would simply drive out of the water, drop the screens and then they would be able to fight entirely normally. The DD concept was originally tested on the Valentine tank from 1941, but by 1944 Shermans were invariably used.

Whether the DD tanks made much difference on D-Day is a debatable issue and relatively few of these were employed. However, a few weeks later a simple improvised modification applied to most of the tanks of US First Army may have made a real difference. This was the Rhino, a set of tusk-like prongs welded to the front of the tank to enable it to cut through hedgerows, rather than being confined by the many high banks that enclosed Normandy's roads.

Heavy Tanks, 1942–5

Among the most fearsome weapons of the war, heavy tanks were equally formidable in action against enemy strong points and armour. With their great gun power some could pick off opposing tanks at well over a kilometre.

At the start of the war the main users of heavy tanks were Britain and the USSR. The British nomenclature "infantry tanks" well described their function for both nations, which was to accompany and support the infantry assault. The far more formidable machines in service in the second half of the war retained this role in part, but their anti-armour performance generally became more important. The tanks included here normally served in separate heavy tank or infantry support units.

Britain's last infantry tank was the Churchill, in service in a range of variants from 1941. The initial version was rushed into service and, as well as being woefully under-gunned (with a 2pdr/40mm), was extremely unreliable at first. Later marks had the 6pdr (57mm), then a 75mm (2.95in). All versions were well-armoured but slow, though they were very good at climbing slopes and crossing obstacles. Over 6,500 of all marks were built, plus several hundred more for specialized engineer tasks.

SOVIET POWER

The performance of the Soviet KV-1 heavy tanks in service in 1941 came as a shock to the Germans but gradually improved German guns meant that they lost their invulnerability later, while their own 76.2mm (3in) weapon was inadequate against newer German tank types. Small numbers of a stop-gap KV-85, with an 85mm (3.35in) gun, were produced in the second half of 1943 before production ended. Some 10,000 of all models were built.

Their replacement was the Josef Stalin series. A few examples of this design were built, each with 85mm and 100mm (3.94in) weapons before a final decision on the 122mm (4.8in) D25 gun was made. This had a slightly poorer armour-piercing performance than the 100mm, but this was compensated for in part by its more powerful high-explosive shell for the other aspects of the tank's role. One definite disadvantage, however, was the

Below: Tiger tanks preparing for an attack on the Eastern Front.

JOSEF STALIN 2

The JS-2 was deliberately kept relatively small – it was no heavier than the KV or the German Panther. Even so, it packed a fearsome punch and had well-sloped armour for effective protection.

WEIGHT: 44.7 tonnes
LENGTH: 8.33m (27ft 4in)
HEIGHT: 2.72m (8ft 11in)
WIDTH: 3.12m (10ft 3in)
ARMOUR: 120mm (4.7in)
ROAD SPEED: 37kph (23mph)
ARMAMENT: 1 x 122mm (4.8in) D25T + 4 x machine-guns

TIGER 2/KÖNIGSTIGER

For all their great fighting power, only 454 Tiger 2s were built, serving in only a handful of heavy-tank battalions. The group shown were photographed for a propaganda film in France in summer 1944.

WEIGHT: 69.4 tonnes
LENGTH: 7.23m (23ft 9in)
HEIGHT: 3.07m (10ft 1in)
WIDTH: 3.73m (12ft 3in)
ARMOUR: 180mm (7.1in)
ROAD SPEED: 35kph (22mph)
ARMAMENT: 1 x 8.8cm (3.46in) KwK 42 + 2 x machine-guns

Above: M26 Pershings of the US 2nd Armored Division in the streets of Magdeburg on the Elbe in 1945.

slow rate of fire of the 122mm and the fact that only 28 rounds could be carried. Probably about 4,000 of the JS-1 and JS-2 variants saw service; a JS-3 version was in production by 1945 but did not see combat.

TIGERS IN ACTION

The first of the German designs that outmatched the KV-1 was the famous PzKpfw 6 Tiger, introduced in September 1942 on the Eastern Front. Design work on the Tiger had begun before Operation Barbarossa revealed the strength of the Soviet armour but was then greatly speeded up. When introduced, the Tiger mounted the then most powerful tank gun in the world (the 8.8cm/3.46in KwK 36) behind very thick armour; it quickly gained a fearsome reputation for its gun power and defensive strength. Mobility and reliability were never strong points, but it was still a tough opponent when the last of 1,355 came off the production line in August 1944.

Its replacement was the Tiger 2 (also know as the Königstiger; 454 built by 1945). It first saw service in Normandy in July 1944. At some 70 tonnes it was massively armoured and its 8.8cm KwK 42 was substantially more powerful than the Tiger 1's gun. Predictably its weak point was its mobility, but in the defensive battles then being mainly fought by the German Army this was not necessarily a great disadvantage.

After delays in the mid-war period, the modest capabilities of the M4 Sherman, in comparison to the German Tigers and Panthers, finally spurred production of something better for the US Army from later in 1944. The M26 Pershing first saw combat in February 1945 and a few hundred were shipped to Europe by VE-Day. It carried an effective 90mm (3.54in) M3 gun and had a good balance of protection and engine power.

Self-propelled Artillery

In a fast-moving war, armoured units needed their artillery to be as mobile as their tanks and a variety of self-propelled guns was developed to fill this role. Most were based on standard field gun weapons but some were in the heavy artillery class.

Weapons in this category are those self-propelled (SP) guns whose armament was designed principally or even exclusively for use with high-explosive or similar ammunition – and which normally lacked the armour protection to allow their regular use within direct-fire range of the enemy.

Designs in this class in both British and American service were regarded as pure artillery weapons, serving in the American case in "armored field artillery regiments" and operating like towed field artillery units with additional mobility. For the Soviet and German Armies the distinction between weapons of this type and those described as assault guns is not always clear-cut.

THE WESTERN ALLIES

The earliest Anglo-American types made their debuts in the Desert War in 1942. The first British design was the Bishop, a 25pdr (87mm) gun mounted in a high box-like superstructure on a Valentine tank chassis. This was not a success – among other faults the mounting greatly limited the gun's elevation, halving its normal range.

The most-produced US design first fought at Alamein in 1942 in British hands. This was the M7 105mm HMC (or Priest in British service). It carried a standard 105mm (4.13in) M2 Howitzer (with restricted elevation, though not as badly as the Bishop) on a chassis based on the M3 Lee tank. It continued in use through 1945. British forces used a similar vehicle, fitted with a full-elevation 25pdr and known as the Sexton.

Other American designs included two light types, mounting 75mm (2.95in) guns. The M3 GMC was mounted on a converted M3 half track and the M8 HMC on a modified M5 Stuart tank chassis. Neither was a great success.

A small number of M12 155mm GMCs, carrying a WWI-era 155mm (6.1in) gun, were used in north-west Europe in 1944–5. Other designs using rather more modern 155mm guns and howitzers were developed but not produced in time to see action.

BISHOP

The need to produce artillery weapons that could keep up with fast-moving tank battles in the Desert War led to the rushed development of the Bishop. About 100 saw action in North Africa, like this one, shown in Tunisia in 1943.

WEIGHT: 17.4 tonnes
LENGTH: 5.53m (18ft 2in)
HEIGHT: 2.76m (9ft 1in)
WIDTH: 2.61m (8ft 7in)
ARMOUR: 60mm (2.4in) max.
ROAD SPEED: 24kph (15mph)
ARMAMENT: 1 x 25pdr (87mm)
  Gun Mark 2; 32 rounds carried

Below: A German Wespe 10.5cm battery with vehicles whitewashed for winter camouflage.

Right: M7 105mm guns in front of Notre Dame during the French 2nd Armoured Division's triumphant liberation of Paris in August 1944.

THE EASTERN FRONT

Soviet designs covered here include several mounting versions of the 152mm (5.98in) gun. The early-war KV-1 heavy tank was accompanied by a 152mm-armed KV-2. This was well-armoured, but its high, boxy shape made it clumsy and vulnerable. The next type, the SU-152, also used the KV chassis but was much more effective, in service from the Battle of Kursk in 1943. Around 700 were built. It was replaced in production in 1944 by the JSU-152, carrying the same weapon but based on the JS-series of heavy tanks. All of these weapons also had a significant anti-tank capability.

German designs were more varied. The Wespe was roughly equivalent to the American M7.

It carried the standard 10.5cm leFh 18 howitzer on a Panzer 2 chassis and was allocated to the artillery units of Panzer divisions. Some 700 were built and served from 1943. Its heavier partner in the Panzer force was the Hummel, fitted with the 15cm (5.91in) sFH 18.

In addition a small number of vehicles on a variety of chassis were built to carry the sIG 33 15cm gun. A further design

(over 300 made) was the Sturmpanzer 4, sometimes known as the Brummbär, a well-armoured type carrying a 15cm StuH 43.

At the other extreme was the Karl Gerät, a 60cm (23.6in) siege mortar mounted on tracks. Six were made and they were provided with alternative 54cm (21.3in) barrels for longer range. The 60cm shell weighed 2,170kg (4,784lb) and could reach 6,580m (7,200yd).

STURMPANZER 4 BRUMMBÄR

The Brummbär ("Grizzly Bear") was an infantry support gun carried on a Panzer 4 chassis. Its 15cm howitzer fired a heavier (38kg/84lb) shell than the earlier StuG 3. It served successfully from 1943 and about 300 were built or converted.

WEIGHT: 28.6 tonnes
LENGTH: 5.93m (19ft 5in)
HEIGHT: 2.52m (8ft 3in)
WIDTH: 2.88m (9ft 5in)
ARMOUR: 100mm (3.9in) max.
ROAD SPEED: 40kph (25mph)
ARMAMENT: 1 x 15cm (5.91in) StuH 43; 38 rounds carried

Unarmoured Vehicles

Fighting armies consumed vast quantities of fuel and ammunition and fighting soldiers naturally needed to be fed. Transport vehicles to achieve these tasks were thus, if anything, more important than fighting equipment.

By the end of June 1944 the Allied forces had landed 150,000 vehicles in Normandy to support the 850,000 men by then deployed. Many of these were armoured fighting vehicles, but many more were soft-skin transport lorries, artillery tractors, repair trucks and other varieties. Another telling statistic is that during the invasion of the USSR in 1941 the Germans employed 2,000 different types of vehicle – and their army was only partly mechanized and still also had hundreds of thousands of draught animals. The importance of motor vehicles is thus obvious, as is the impossibility of detailing more than a sample of those used.

Probably the most famous transport vehicle of the war was the Jeep, originally designed by the Willys company and built mainly by Ford. To the US Army it was the "Truck ¼-ton, 4 x 4". Over 600,000 were made and many supplied to almost every Allied nation, in addition to their use with US forces. And as well as these there were vast numbers of ½-ton and ¾-ton vehicles from Ford, Dodge, Chevrolet and others in the light-truck class.

Other countries had equivalent equipment. The Soviets built GAZ-67 copies of the Jeep to supplement their Lend-Lease supplies. The Germans had the Kübelwagen, based on the original pre-war Volkswagen design. Even the Italians had a Fiat 508 type, which was used effectively in North Africa.

ARTILLERY TRACTORS

Jeeps were often used to tow anti-tank guns but all nations had specialized designs for the artillery-tractor role. British 25pdr guns were often towed by Morris C8 "Quad" tractors and heavier weapons by AEC Matadors. US heavy artillery units used several models of fully-tracked vehicle in the same role, which were surprisingly fast and had good cross-country capabilities. Many of these were made by the Allis-Chalmers company, previously known for its farm tractors.

Left: An American truck convoy on the Red Ball Express route in France in 1944.

Above: Tractors pull Soviet heavy artillery guns during the advance to Berlin in early 1945.

Soviet heavy artillery units also employed tracked vehicles produced by the tractor industry. German heavy towing vehicles included SdKfz 8 and 9 half tracks, which could also be used for tank-recovery duties.

Moving tanks to and from the battle area and recovering damaged ones in the field was a highly important support role. American tank-transporter types, also used by the British, included vehicles by Diamond T and Mack, while native British types included examples from Albion and Scammel.

CARGO VEHICLES

For simple cargo-carrying duties the USA's 2½-ton ("deuce and a half") design stands out. A truly massive 800,000 were built, mostly by General Motors, and they were supplied to all the Allies. By the end of the war the Soviets had more American trucks in use on the Eastern Front than indigenous ones.

Most countries had equivalent designs of roughly 3-tonne capacity, made by their own famous motor manufacturers, and usually a smaller number of larger vehicles up to the 10-tonne or 12-tonne class. Examples included Britain's 10-tonne Leyland Hippo or the Soviet YAG-10, an 8-tonne design.

Above: A Scammel tank transporter leads a British column in the advance after El Alamein in 1942.

The best-known use of transport lorries in the war was in the so-called Red Ball Express, set up by the Allied forces in France during 1944 in a desperate attempt to keep their advancing forces supplied. This used several thousand trucks running on a loop of one-way roads between St-Lô and Chartres. However, even this vast effort could not keep the armies going by mid-September 1944, when they were upward of 700km (435 miles) from the Normandy beaches, where their supplies were being landed.

TRANSPORT ANIMALS

The degree to which armies were mechanized varied considerably. Britain and the USA used motor transport whenever possible but in 1941, for example, the German Army had over 600,000 horses participating in Operation Barbarossa. In the course of the war the USSR probably lost 14 million horses, though many of these would not have been working with the Red Army. Even the British and Americans made significant use of transport animals, mainly mules, in particularly difficult terrain in Sicily, Italy and Burma. And over 1,000 elephants were used by the Allied forces in Burma.

Above: German transport crossing a river in Russia.

Heavy Mortars and Artillery Rockets

Germany's Nebelwerfer and the Soviet Katyusha were among the most-feared land weapons of WWII. Heavy mortars, too, generated awesome firepower concentrations and caused many casualties.

Heavy mortars and ground-to-ground rockets produced some of the most devastating sudden bombardments of the war. Rockets and mortars in fact had advantages over traditional artillery guns. They could bring down a heavy volume of fire quickly and fairly accurately on a target; and the more nearly vertical trajectory of their shells ensured that their fragmentation pattern was highly effective. More than half of the British casualties in north-west Europe in 1944–5 were inflicted by these weapons, for example.

In addition to the mortars used for infantry support, most armies also had heavier types, but the Germans and Soviets

Below: A Soviet 120mm (4.72in) mortar battery in action in the streets of Berlin at the end of the war.

made most use of these. The Soviet 120mm (4.72in) HM38 (based on a French Brandt design) fired a 16kg (35lb) bomb up to 6,000m (6,500yd). Other Soviet weapons were 160mm (6.3in) and 240mm (9.45in) designs. The German 12cm (4.72in) design was a copy of the Soviet HM38. The USA and Britain both used 4.2in (107mm) weapons. The American type was unusual in having a rifled barrel; most other mortars were smoothbore weapons.

Rocket Artillery

The Soviets and the Germans made more extensive use than other armies of rocket artillery. The German Nebelwerfer types included 6-tube 15cm (5.91in) and 5-tube 21cm (8.27in) designs as well as larger calibres. The Soviet Katyushas were

often truck mounted and included the M8 firing 32 x 82mm (3.23in) rockets and the M13 firing 16 x 132mm (5.2in) rockets. These latter had an 18kg (40lb) warhead and could reach a range of 8,500m (9,300yd).

Rocket weapons often had a distinctive noise when fired: Anglo-American troops knew the Nebelwerfer types as "Moaning Minnies"; Red Army troops called their Katyushas "Stalin's Organs".

SdKfz 4/1 MAULTIER

The SdKfz 4 was a half-track version of Germany's standard 3-tonne trucks. It was designed to cope with difficult ground on the Eastern Front. About 300 were built to carry Panzerwerfer 42 rocket launchers.

WEIGHT: 7.1 tonnes
LENGTH: 6m (19ft 8in)
HEIGHT: 2.5m (8ft 2in)
ARMOUR: 8mm (0.3in)
ROAD SPEED: 40kph (25mph)
ARMAMENT: 10 x 15cm (5.91in) Panzerwerfer 42 rockets

V-Weapons

*Hitler thought that these "Retaliation Weapons" would win the war for Germany,
but despite their sinister reputation their effectiveness was more limited.
Producing them also cost the lives of thousands of slave labourers.*

Cruise missiles and ballistic missiles are part of the everyday military vocabulary of the 21st century; their ultimate ancestors were the German Fi-103 and A-4, which saw much use in WWII. Both types had a variety of codenames and designations: most are commonly known by the V designation (V for *Vergeltungswaffe*, or "retaliation weapon"), first coined by German propaganda and then officially endorsed by Hitler.

FIESELER 103/V-1

FUSELAGE LENGTH: 6.65m
(21ft 10in)
WINGSPAN: 5.33m (17ft 6in)
ENGINE: Argus 109-014 pulse
jet; 310kg (680lb) max. thrust
MAX. SPEED: 670kph (415mph)
MAX. RANGE: 200km (125 miles)
WARHEAD: 850kg (1,870lb)

V-1 FLYING BOMB
The Fieseler 103, or V-1 flying bomb, was a small pilotless aircraft powered by a pulse-jet engine, fitted with an auto-pilot to guide it to its target. Tested from 1942, it was put into action in June 1944, a few days after the D-Day landings.

In the early stages most of the missiles fired were targeted on London. Of the roughly 8,600 launched before the French bases were overrun by the Allied armies, about a quarter reached their targets. Later in the war Antwerp and other Belgian cities were targeted, again with modest accuracy; about half of the missiles launched landed within a dozen kilometres of their targets.

Although the V-1 was cheap to make (around 5,000 marks each, 2.5 per cent of the price of a V-2), the 30,000 made took up more than half of German explosives production in 1944–5 and inflicted fewer than 7,000 fatalities on the British people.

V-2 ROCKET
The A-4/V-2 ballistic missile was an altogether more high-tech weapon. Its liquid-fuel rocket carried it 80km (50 miles) into the stratosphere before it fell at supersonic speed onto its target. Unlike the V-1 it could not be intercepted by fighter aircraft or anti-aircraft gunfire.

About 3,500 were fired at London and other cities from September 1944, carrying in all less explosive power than a single large Allied bombing raid on Germany in the same period. More slave labourers died in the Nazi factories making the V-2 than were killed by the missile attacks. With a more powerful warhead, the story might have been different. However, in this vein, it has also been calculated that the development cost of the V-2 was about the same as the American expenditure in making the atom bomb.

A-4C/V-2

LENGTH: 14m (45ft 11in)
FUSELAGE DIAMETER: 1.64m
(5ft 5in)
ENGINE: Liquid-fuel rocket
FLIGHT TIME: 330 seconds
MAX. RANGE: 314km (195 miles)
WARHEAD: 730–975kg
(1,600–2,150lb)

Anti-tank Guns, 1942–5

Higher muzzle velocities and new types of ammunition ensured that anti-tank guns still posed a formidable threat to even the monster heavy tanks produced for the final battles of the war.

The increase in power seen in anti-tank guns of the early-war years continued during the second half of the war, though with the improvements being derived more from new types of ammunition rather than large increases in calibre. Armies also found that towed anti-tank guns in the larger calibres could be clumsy in action and more difficult to conceal; accordingly they turned increasingly to self-propelled (SP) weapons in the anti-tank role.

NEW AMMUNITION

In ammunition, simple solid-shot armour-piercing (AP) designs were found to be prone to shattering on impact, because of the higher velocities being used. They were also more likely to glance off the sloped armour that more and more tanks included. This led to the introduction of capped rounds (APC) to achieve better impacts and ballistic caps on top of these (APCBC) to restore ideal shapes.

Composite rounds with a dense penetrating core encased in a lighter carrier (armour-piercing composite rigid – APCR; or high velocity armour-piercing in the US designation – HVAP) were also introduced, as well as a better version of these in which the light carrier fell away on leaving the barrel (armour-piercing discarding sabot – APDS). These had an ideal combination of lightness to accelerate quickly in the gun barrel but with a hard and dense munition with good carrying power, penetration and accuracy. Various guns had a different range of ammunition developed at different times during the

Below: A 17pdr (76mm) anti-tank gun of the 2nd New Zealand Division in action at Monte Cassino in Italy in early 1944.

NASHORN

The Nashorn ("Rhinoceros"; also known as the Hornisse, or "Hornet") was a very effective tank destroyer armed with the long-barrel 8.8cm gun. The basic vehicle was a modified Panzer 4 chassis. It was first used at Kursk in 1943.

WEIGHT: 24 tonnes
LENGTH: 7.17m (23ft 6in)
HEIGHT: 2.65m (8ft 8in)
WIDTH: 2.8m (9ft 2in)
ARMOUR: 30mm (1.2in) max.
ROAD SPEED: 42kph (26mph)
ARMAMENT: 1 x 8.8cm (3.46in) PaK 43; 25 rounds carried

Right: American infantry pass a pair of knocked-out Hetzer tank destroyers. The Hetzer was built on the old PzKpfw 38(t) chassis.

war; APDS was a British speciality introduced for the 6pdr (57mm) in the spring of 1944, for example.

Earlier weapons like the 6pdr remained in use to the end of the war, in part thanks to improved ammunition, but also because they could still be effective against most opponents at shorter ranges. In British service, however, the 6pdr was supplemented from 1942 by the 17pdr (76mm). The essentially identical US 57mm was supplemented by the 3in (76mm) M5 and the dual-purpose version of the 90mm (3.54in), originally made as an anti-aircraft gun.

SELF-PROPELLED GUNS

All of these weapons featured on SP mounts. Indeed the towed and SP guns served together in the American tank-destroyer units. The most notable of these were the M10 (with the 3in gun) and the M36 (90mm), as well as a lighter, faster design, the M18 Hellcat, which mounted the same 76mm weapon as later US Sherman tanks. For Britain, the 17pdr gun was mounted in an M10 variant – the Achilles – and in a vehicle derived from the Valentine tank – the Archer.

Soviet anti-tank weapons included the ZiS-3 76.2mm (3in) field gun, which had a respectable AP performance. This gun was made by the tens of thousands, along with the very formidable 100mm (3.94in) BS-3 introduced in 1944. Most

Soviet SP guns with a significant anti-tank capability were more heavily armoured SU-series assault guns.

As well as its assault guns, Germany also had various *Panzerjäger* (or "tank-hunter") types, as well as towed weapons of course. The 7.5cm (2.95in) PaK 40 towed gun was introduced in late 1941 and served to the end of the war. There was also an improved version of the "Eighty-eight" – the 71-calibre 8.8cm (3.46in) PaK 43.

The *Panzerjäger* vehicles included several types known as the Marder. These were based on a variety of chassis and armed with either the German PaK 40 gun or captured Soviet 76.2mm weapons. They were introduced in 1942–3. The later Hetzer was the most numerous *Panzerjäger*, with some 2,500 produced, and also carried a 7.5cm gun. The Nashorn was more formidable, carrying the long-barrelled PaK 43, but only some 500 were made.

M36 GMC

The M36 Gun Motor Carriage entered service in 1944. Several variants existed, built with different engines and hulls. All carried the anti-tank version of the 90mm anti-aircraft gun and could defeat Panther or Tiger tanks.

WEIGHT: 28.1 tonnes
LENGTH: 6.15m (20ft 2in)
HEIGHT: 2.72m (8ft 11in)
WIDTH: 3.04m (10ft)
ARMOUR: 50mm (2in) max.
ROAD SPEED: 48kph (30mph)
ARMAMENT: 1 x 90mm (3.54in) M3; 47 rounds carried

Infantry Anti-tank Weapons

By 1945 infantrymen in the best-equipped armies had man-portable weapons that could destroy even the heaviest tank – if they were brave enough to get desperately close to the metal monsters.

Specially powerful rifles had been used as anti-tank weapons almost from the moment tanks were introduced in WWI. Versions of these were still in service when WWII broke out but were soon made obsolete by improvements in tank armour.

From 1942–3, Britain, the USA and Germany introduced weapons using the hollow-charge principle to focus explosive power. These gave the infantry weapons that could kill a tank, or smash open a pillbox or other fortification.

ANTI-TANK RIFLES

In the early-war years anti-tank rifles in service included the British Boys type, in 0.55in (14mm) calibre, and two Soviet designs – the PTRD 1941 and PTRS 1941 – both in 14.55mm (0.57in) calibre. These all had

Above: A young German soldier waits in a ruined house with his Panzerfaust at the ready.

similar performance, being capable of penetrating some 25mm (1in) of armour at 400m (440yd). Smaller-calibre types included the Polish Maroszek Wz 35 (also used in significant

numbers by the Italians) and the German Panzerbüsche 38 and 39, all in 7.92mm (0.312in).

ROCKET LAUNCHERS

The US Army had no anti-tank rifle when it entered the war but soon acquired something better – the 2.36in (60mm) M1 Rocket Launcher (called the Bazooka). This could destroy most contemporary Axis tanks and had a range of up to 400m (440yd), though accuracy at this distance was far from certain. Later versions had the calibre increased to 3in (76.2mm) with improved armour-piercing performance.

Germany's 8.8cm (3.46in) Panzerschreck (or "Tank Terror") was essentially a copy of the Bazooka. Britain's Projector Infantry Anti-Tank (PIAT) looked clumsy and primitive, but it was able to fire a useful 1.4kg (3.1lb) bomb.

Germany also used the even more innovative Panzerfaust (or "Tank Fist"), a light and simple single-shot weapon with the firing tube designed to be discarded after use. The longest-range Panzerfaust variant could only reach 100m (110yd), but its power and ease of use made it a formidable threat to any tank, especially in close country or a built-up area.

No other army developed such weapons during WWII.

Left: Later in the war the Soviets often used anti-tank rifles, as here, against enemy positions, not tanks.

Mines and Other Defences

Mines, and their close relatives booby traps, are sometimes called silent soldiers, lying patiently in wait for an enemy. They were a threat on every battlefield of the war, capable of killing in battle and long after fighting had moved elsewhere.

There were two main categories of mine that were in use during WWII – anti-personnel and anti-tank – the former usually being smaller and requiring a lighter force to set them off, the latter larger and heavier. Minefields could be set in any open area and contain one, or more often both, types; and individual or small numbers of mines could be used for point defence or as booby traps virtually anywhere.

Troops hated enemy mines, with some justification. Anti-personnel mines were often designed more to maim than to kill, since a wounded soldier often got assistance, taking perhaps several combatants out of the firing line.

The design of mines also often inspired fear. Both Germany and the USA used mines that had two charges – one to throw the mine into the air when it was disturbed; and a second main charge to detonate it there. Germany's Schrapnellmine, for example, blasted out some 350 shrapnel balls from a position roughly 1.5m (5ft) above ground, with devastating effect.

Anti-tank mines could be both bar- and discus-shaped. The Italian forces were the first to use them, in the Western Desert in 1940. Common designs included the Soviet TM/39 which carried a 3kg (6.6lb) charge or the slightly heavier British Mark V.

Germany and the USSR were the most prolific users of mines. As well as the most often encountered Tellermine anti-tank designs, Germany also had a variety of anti-tank and anti-personnel types in glass, plastic and wooden cases, all designed to make detection harder. Many mines of all nations were also fitted with anti lifting devices to make their removal more difficult and dangerous.

Above: A Canadian engineer preparing to clear an enemy anti-tank mine in Italy.

Right: Soviet engineers laying mines to block a German advance on the Eastern Front in 1942.

Landing Craft and Amphibious Vehicles

Amphibious vehicles and the many kinds of larger landing craft were vital to the Anglo-American war effort. Without them the whole counter-offensive in the Pacific and the defeat of Germany in western Europe would have been impossible.

Although amphibious opera-tions had a long history, as late as a 1938 exercise (led by a certain Brigadier Montgomery) British troops were mainly using rowing boats to get ashore.

By then, however, the Japanese had a purpose-built 8,000-ton landing ship in service – the *Shinshu Maru* – which could deploy new Daihatsu landing craft from the stern. Japan subsequently introduced a small number of additional landing ships and landing craft, employing them successfully in its early offensive campaigns. In addition there were a few Toyota SUKI amphibious trucks in service, too.

US MARINE IDEAS

The other pioneer in landing operations was the US Marine Corps. In the inter-war period the Marines developed many of the ideas on amphibious warfare that would be put into action in WWII. In 1938 they began tests on so-called Higgins boats (in part copied from Daihatsu types seen in action in China). The wooden Higgins boats would be developed into more robust metal Landing Craft, Vehicle, personnel (LCVP), used by the

Below: US Army troops aboard an LCVP heading for Omaha Beach on D-Day. An LCVP typically carried 36 troops and 3 crew.

LCT MARK V

Several designs of Landing Craft Tank were built in Britain and the US from November 1940. The Mark V was a US design. This example is shown during operations on Rendova Island in the New Georgia group during 1943.

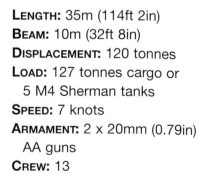

LENGTH: 35m (114ft 2in)
BEAM: 10m (32ft 8in)
DISPLACEMENT: 120 tonnes
LOAD: 127 tonnes cargo or 5 M4 Sherman tanks
SPEED: 7 knots
ARMAMENT: 2 x 20mm (0.79in) AA guns
CREW: 13

thousand in many WWII cam-paigns. In 1941 the Marines also ordered the first of the impor-tant Landing Vehicle Tracked (LVT) series of amphibians. Later LVTs could carry 3 tonnes of cargo and be armed with weapons as large as a 75mm (2.95in) howitzer. Over 18,000 were built.

Even more prolifically produced was the DUKW amphibious truck. A final American amphibian was the smaller Studebaker M29 Weasel cargo carrier. All these amphibians were also used by the British.

BRITISH TYPES

By 1940 Britain had a small number of Landing Craft Assault (LCA) and Landing Craft Mechanized (LCM) in service – capable of carrying an infantry platoon or a tank, respectively – and soon added a number of other types. There was more than one variety of Landing Ship Infantry (LSI), converted either from ferries or small liners, and purpose-built Landing Ships Dock (LSD).

Rough American equivalents were Auxiliary Personnel Attack (APA) ships and Attack Cargo (AKA) ships. These various "ships" were not designed to reach all the way to landing beaches themselves but carried smaller "craft" into which they would load troops and supplies for the assault landings.

Also designed in Britain from 1940 – and subsequently made in large numbers in the USA – were various marks of Landing Craft Tank (LCT). The largest were around 56m (185ft) long and could carry nine Sherman tanks, landing them from a ramp at the bow.

These landing craft were among the smallest of a variety of types made for so-called shore-to-shore operations. They would be loaded in friendly territory and then sail under their own power to the landing area. Such vessels included Landing Ships Tank (LST) and Landing Craft Infantry, Large

Above: In the later stages of the Pacific war many Japanese landing craft, like this one on Saipan, were destroyed while trying to support island garrisons under attack.

(LCI/L); around a thousand of each were built. An LST could carry some 20 tanks and an LCI/L 180–210 infantrymen.

OTHER USES

Many landing vessels of all sizes were converted to specialized uses. Some became command or hospital vessels and others gave covering anti-aircraft fire. The most spectacular were the rocket-armed versions, which could fire a devastating barrage of up to 1,000 rockets into a landing area. By 1945 the variety and sophistication of landing craft and their tactics, and the weight of fire support available, meant that an assault landing could be made successfully against almost any opposition – hence the Japanese decision on Okinawa not to oppose the American landings at all.

DUKW

The DUKW amphibian was a 6 x 6 on land, based on a 2.5-tonne General Motors truck. It was used by the thousand in all theatres to unload transport ships and carry their cargoes inland to the troops. The examples shown are in British service preparing for D-Day.

LENGTH: 9.45m (31ft)
WIDTH: 2.49m (8ft 2in)
WEIGHT: 6.7 tonnes + 2.3 tonnes cargo
ENGINE: 91.5hp GMC
SPEED: 80kph (50mph) land; 10kph (6.2mph) water

Weapons of Mass Destruction

Although thousands had died from the effects of poison gas in WWI and cities were razed to the ground by conventional bombing attacks in WWII, the atomic, chemical and biological weapons developed by 1945 were a new and more terrible threat.

By the late 1930s scientists were familiar with the idea that chain reactions might be created in certain elements to give off vast amounts of energy that could conceivably be used in some type of bomb.

Scientists in Japan and the USSR were among those who realized this possibility, but neither of those countries pursued the idea at that stage – and American research was not then extensive.

Britain, however, took things further. Rudolph Peierls and Otto Frisch, Jewish refugees from the Nazis, made the breakthrough; they calculated that a relatively small quantity of the rare uranium 235 isotope would be needed for a bomb. (Ironically, the two were only working in this field because they were not yet fully trusted to join native British scientists in "more vital" electronics and radar research.) Other scientists, in Britain and the USA, also

Above: General Leslie Groves (right) and J. R. Oppenheimer, respectively military head and chief scientist of the Manhattan Project.

worked out a second method of "bomb-making". This involved the creation of a new element – plutonium – from the common uranium 238 isotope.

THE FIRST A-BOMBS

British developments were shared with the Americans, who began more serious work in late 1941. This soon developed into the huge Manhattan Project, to which the British scientists were transferred. By early 1945 both U235 and plutonium were being produced in sufficient quantities and two designs of bomb were being finalized.

On 16 July 1945 a plutonium device was exploded in a test at Alamogordo, New Mexico. Its yield was calculated as equivalent to at least 15,000 tonnes of TNT; the explosion was visible and audible up to 275km (170 miles) away. The bomb dropped on Nagasaki, known as "Fat Man", was a second plutonium weapon. The Hiroshima device, "Little Boy", was based on the U235 isotope.

Although the greatest motivation in starting the research was to forestall German development of similar weapons, US leaders soon realized that the unprecedented power of atomic weapons could transform international affairs. Ideas that Japan be given a demonstration of the bomb's power before it was used were never taken seriously. With Allied lives at stake, there was never any question that the bomb would be used in action as soon as possible.

GASES AND POISONS

WWII also saw developments in chemical and biological warfare. Fortunately such weapons were little used, mainly from fear that any use would bring equivalent retaliation and therefore gain nothing. However, it was a great relief to Allied

Below: The two atomic bombs used against Japan in 1945. "Little Boy" dropped on Hiroshima (right), and "Fat Man", the Nagasaki weapon (left).

Above: "Be prepared to ward off chemical weapons" – a Soviet poster from WWII.

HEAVY WATER

One method of making plutonium used so-called "heavy water" (a compound featuring the hydrogen isotope deuterium), for which the best source under German control was a hydroelectric plant at Rjukan in Norway. British and Norwegian special forces sabotaged the plant in 1943 and in 1944 prevented its production reaching Germany. By then, unknown to the Allies, Germany's atomic research had been effectively abandoned because the amount of U235 needed for a bomb had been miscalculated.

leaders that Germany's V-weapons had only conventional explosive warheads.

All nations took precautions against the use of poison gas, as they had in WWI. Gas masks were issued to troops and civilians; generally stocks of WWI gases like mustard gas and phosgene were ready for retaliatory use. Italy employed mustard gas in its conquest of Abyssinia, but such weapons were not used otherwise in WWII. Germany alone developed nerve gases – tabun and sarin – but did not deploy them. This research fell into Soviet hands in 1945.

Several countries experimented with biological agents and produced weapons to use them, though Hitler forbade such research in Germany. Both Britain and the USA had anthrax and botulin weapons ready by the end of the war, but only Japan used weapons of this type. The Japanese researchers (known as Unit 731 and com-manded by General Ishii Shiro) killed many hundreds of Chinese prisoners of war in experiments in this field. They made successful attempts to spread diseases like cholera, typhoid and plague against the Chinese forces, notably in 1942 in Kiangsi province.

Above: Governments took the threat of chemical attack seriously as this 1943 British exercise shows.

Ishii and his team were captured by the Americans in 1945 and given immunity from prosecution in return for information about their research.

AIR FORCE WEAPONS

World War II saw the use of air power to a level far beyond anything previously attempted. Developments in radio and electronics meant that air operations could be directed, and radar could detect aircrafts hundreds of miles away. Fighters and bombers became more heavily armed, and better tactics were practised.

Image: A late war example of the Spitfire MkXIV with griffin engine, pictured on an English airfield.

Light Bombers, Recce and Utility Aircraft

*Modest armament fits, or even none at all, were the hallmarks of these aircraft types.
Paradoxically, perhaps, the least successful of these designs were the light bombers –
the unarmed reconnaissance and utility types had a far lower casualty rate.*

The light bomber category included a number of designs in service in 1939 but most of these were soon found seriously wanting. They were replaced by either the heavier bombers or by purpose-built ground-attack machines.

LIGHT BOMBER DESIGNS

Britain and France both had aircraft of this type in 1939–40. The Fairey Battle had seemed a capable design when it entered service in 1937, but by 1940 its low speed and non-existent armour protection made it, in effect, a deathtrap.

France's Potez 63 series had similar faults and the Breguet 691 was little better, though it did have a more substantial defensive armament. The Bloch

Above: Some 800 examples of the Fw 189 Uhu were used as ground-attack and reconnaissance aircraft.

Below: A Fieseler Storch shows its ability to land (and take off) from unconventional airfields, in this case a Berlin boulevard.

174 was fast (530kph/329mph) and carried a useful 400kg (880lb) bomb load, but only 50 were in service in May 1940. As also to some extent in Britain, the profusion of relatively small French aircraft companies prevented sufficient development

MITSUBISHI Ki-46

The Mitsubishi Ki-46 entered service with the Japanese Army in 1940. It remained in use to 1945, latterly and unsuccessfully as a fighter (shown below), armed with 2 x 20mm (0.79in) cannon in the nose and 1 x 37mm (1.46in) upward-firing gun.

SPEED: 600kph (375mph)
RANGE: 4,000km (2,500 miles)
CREW: 2
ENGINES: 2 x Mitsubishi Ha-102 radials; 1,080hp each
ARMAMENT: 1 x 7.7mm (0.303in) machine-gun

and production effort being given in the pre-war period to the best designs.

Early-war Soviet Sukhoi 2s had similar performance to the above Anglo-French types, with the advantage of reasonable armour protection for the crew. However, many were still shot down by the superior Luftwaffe fighters of 1941.

Although these "modern" designs proved short-lived, some seemingly less capable aircraft (many of them biplanes) fought on in night harassment and similar roles. Aircraft in this category included the Soviet Polikarpov I-153 (originally designed as a fighter) and the German

Henschel 123 (built specifically for the attack role). Less capable was the Czech Letov S328, dating back to 1933, still used by some of the Eastern Front's minor air forces in 1944–5.

RECONNAISSANCE

Many well-known aircraft types had variants produced to serve in the reconnaissance role. In the British case specialized versions of both the Spitfire and Mosquito were built for this purpose. Usually, they were unarmed and fitted with uprated engines, along with appropriate cameras for planned high- or low-level missions. The American equivalents included modified Lightning fighters and Havoc bombers. Some designs were given pressurized cabins and other fittings to help them achieve extreme altitudes where they would be very difficult to intercept.

Only one land-based aircraft type was built specifically for the long-range reconnaissance role: Japan's Mitsubishi Ki-46 "Dinah". Over 1,700 of this design were produced and could reach over 600kph (375mph). Range was an impressive 4,000km (2,485 miles).

One of the few aircraft that specialized in the tactical reconnaissance role was Germany's Focke-Wulf 189, which served extensively on the Eastern Front. It was comparatively slow but survived through its toughness and extreme agility.

UTILITY DESIGNS

Most nations had small light transport aircraft, which were also employed for such tasks as artillery spotting and landing agents in enemy territory.

POTEZ 63-11

The Potez 63 family included several bomber, fighter and reconnaissance variants. The 63-11 shown was used mainly in reconnaissance, with about 700 being built, including some for the Vichy air force. Potez 633 bombers served with Romania and Greece.

SPEED: 439kph (273mph)
RANGE: 1,300km (800 miles)
CREW: 3
ENGINES: 2 x Gnome Rhône 14M radials; 700hp each
ARMAMENT: 200kg (440lb) bombs; 3 x machine-guns

These could be found in either army or air force service, according to nationality. General Rommel famously used one such type, a Fieseler Storch, in flights over the North African battlefields, landing from time to time to chivvy on lagging subordinates. Britain's Westland Lysander regularly flew covert missions carrying resistance personnel into France. American equivalents included the Taylorcraft L-2 Grasshopper. The one crucial performance attribute of such aircraft was usually their ability to take off and land in confined and rough areas. None were fast or ever more than lightly armed.

Fighters, 1939–42

In 1940 in the Battle of Britain, the fate of the world depended to a significant degree on the qualities of the two sides' Spitfire, Hurricane and Messerschmitt fighters. Air combat superiority was vital in this and every other campaign.

Like every other kind of military technology, fighters had to have a balance of usually conflicting qualities: speed, rate of climb, manoeuvrability, range, armament, protection and others. Most fighters in service throughout the war were single-piston-engined, pilot-only, low-wing monoplanes. A few biplanes and twin-engined monoplane designs were also produced but generally saw little combat as day fighters.

BIPLANES

Some countries with good modern designs still had a number of biplanes in action in 1939: examples being Germany's Heinkel 51 and Britain's Gloster Gladiator. Typically, they were slow and lightly armed – 400kph (250mph) and four rifle-calibre machine-guns for the Gladiator – and came off badly if facing monoplane opponents. Italy, however, had quite significant numbers of Fiat CR 32 and CR 42 biplanes, and some even continued in use until Italy's surrender in 1943.

MONOPLANES

The classic designs of the era were the Spitfire, Hurricane and Messerschmitt Bf 109. All first flew in 1935–6 and would continue in combat service, albeit in greatly modified forms, until the end of the war. The Spitfire 1 was slightly faster than the Bf 109E (the main versions in service in 1940) and the Hurricane slower than both the others. Both British fighters were more manoeuvrable than the Bf 109, but their 8 x 0.303in (7.7mm) machine-guns were less effective than the Messerschmitt's 2 x 20mm (0.79in) cannon and 2 x 7.92mm (0.312in) machine-guns. Messerschmitts also had a better rate of climb.

Below: A USAAF Curtiss P-40. Many of the 13,700 P-40s built served in the war against Japan.

In 1941 the successor 109F was superior to the Spitfire 5, a balance redressed by the later Spitfire 9. Ultimately, though, there was sufficiently little to choose between them that encounters were more often decided by pilot skill and tactics.

Fighters were not a pre-war priority for the US Army Air Force (USAAF) – after all, there was no possibility of air attacks against the American continent.

POLIKARPOV I-16

The Polikarpov I-16 (shown below) served successfully in Spain before the war. It had a good rate of climb and manoeuvrability and was, in some variants, the best-armed fighter anywhere. It made up about half of the Soviet fighter strength in 1941.

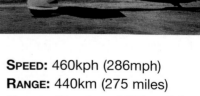

SPEED: 460kph (286mph)
RANGE: 440km (275 miles)
ENGINE: Shvetsov M25 radial; 700hp
ARMAMENT: 2 x 20mm (0.79in) cannon; 2 x 7.62mm (0.3in) machine-guns

Right: A cannon-armed Spitfire 5b of 303 Squadron, a Polish-crewed unit, in flight in 1942.

The Curtiss P-36 and P-40 had modest capabilities but saw significant service with Britain and France. The P-40 was used extensively by British forces in North Africa in slightly different Kittyhawk and Tomahawk forms, but it could never quite compete with the Bf 109. Later-war USAAF fighters were of much higher quality.

Early Soviet fighters were a mixed bag, made worse by low manufacturing standards and poor pilot training. The mid-1930s' Polikarpov I-16 saw extensive use against Finland and in the early days of Operation Barbarossa. It was reasonably well armed but slow by the standards of 1941. The LaGG-1 and -3 were unusual in being built largely of wood and proved to be rugged but again rather slow in combat service.

The Soviets' MiG design bureau produced the MiG-1 and -3 that were most effective at high altitudes (which must have been an ordeal in the MiG-1's open cockpit), but they were otherwise disappointing. Most important were the various Yak designs. The series reached the Yak-7 variant by 1942 and would see further highly successful development later on in the war.

Japanese Army fighters of the early war years showed the same characteristics as the better known "Zero" of the Navy (which also served extensively over land). Their excellent manoeuvrability stood them in good stead when faced with the older designs that the Allies

deployed to the Pacific in 1941–2. However, their weaknesses of light construction and inadequate protection for pilot and fuel tanks proved more important against upgraded opposition later. Notable types included the Nakajima Ki-43 "Oscar" and Ki-44 "Tojo".

TWIN-ENGINED TYPES

Perhaps the only twin-engined day fighter to serve successfully was the Lockheed P-38 Lightning, in use from 1941. Its speed and good range meant it

performed well in the bomber-escort role. Other types like the Bristol Beaufighter or the Messerschmitt 110 lacked the agility that was needed for daytime air combat but appeared in other roles in due course.

DEWOITINE D.520

The Dewoitine D.520 was the best French fighter in 1940. Production failures meant that only 100 were available by May. They fought well in the Battle of France and were later briefly used against the Allies by the Vichy forces in Syria. About 900 were built in all.

SPEED: 535kph (332mph)
RANGE: 1,250km (780 miles)
ENGINE: Hispano-Suiza 12Y45 in-line; 910hp
ARMAMENT: 1 x 20mm (0.79in) cannon, 4 x 7.5mm (0.295in) machine-guns

Air Combat: Weapons, Tactics and Aces

Some pre-war theorists thought air combats were a thing of the past because of the increased speed of aircraft. Instead, sudden dogfights and extended air battles took place in every theatre and air aces became as famous as their WWI predecessors.

Aircraft performance was far from being the only determinant of air combat success during WWII. Fighters and bombers both became more heavily armed as the war proceeded and better tactics were developed and practised.

GUNS AND GUNNERY

Most of the air-to-air weapons in use in 1939 were rifle-calibre (approximately 7.7mm/0.303in) machine-guns. Some fighters, like Italy's CR 42, carried as few as two such weapons, and bombers, like Germany's Heinkel 111, might have only three, in hand-held mounts. Experience soon showed that this was inadequate. The speed

Above: A hand-trained Vickers K machine-gun, the sole defensive weapon fitted to the Fairey Battle.

of air combats and the fleeting moments when an enemy would be in the gunsight made greater firepower essential.

Britain had realized that something better would be needed to shoot down German bombers. Initially, the Spitfire and Hurricane were fitted with eight machine-guns but this was

also shown to be insufficient because the individual rounds had too little striking power.

Alternatives to the rifle-calibre weapons were heavy machine-guns in the 13mm (0.51in) class and even more powerful but slower-firing 20mm (0.79in) cannon and some still bigger guns. Late-war American fighters generally carried six or eight 0.5in (12.7mm) guns and found this adequate. The Germans, facing numerous Allied heavy bombers, favoured a heavier punch, with weapons fits including 3cm (1.18in) cannon and even 21cm (8.27in) unguided air-to-air rockets.

Late-war bombers like the B-17G Flying Fortress might carry up to 13 x 0.5in (12.7mm) machine-guns in a mix of powered turrets and single mounts, but even that was not enough unless the aircraft also flew in a tight formation with its squadron-mates. The B-29 Superfortress took things a stage further with various of its turrets being remotely controlled, not individually manned.

COMBAT TACTICS

At the start of the war, Britain's Fighter Command instructed its fighter squadrons to use tight formations and planned sequences of manoeuvres to attack enemy bombers. This was soon found to be dangerous and impractical. Shortly, all air forces were using the methods developed by the Germans, in

Below: Loading the nose-mounted 0.79in (20mm) cannon in an RAF Bell P-39 Airacobra in 1941.

Right: Ball turret gunners on B-17s (twin 0.5in/12.7mm guns) were all small men for obvious reasons.

particular, in their involvement in the Spanish Civil War – the pair and the finger-four.

The basic unit was made up of a leader and his wingman. They kept relatively close together, with the leader responsible for the tactical decisions and most attacks, while the wingman's principal duty was to make sure they were not surprised from the rear. Two such pairs made up what the RAF called the finger-four, so-called because this group would fly in a loose formation shaped like the spread fingertips of the hand.

AIR ACES

As in WWI, pilots in all countries kept count of their "kills" and successful pilots were celebrated as aces, or in the rather more descriptive German term, *Experten*. Different air forces had varying methods of assessing air combat successes and it is certainly true that pilots generally claimed far more enemy aircraft shot down than were ever actually lost. This was probably as much a product of the speed and confusion of air battle as any deliberate attempt to mislead. However, it is also true that detailed examination of some aces' claims has backed up most of their scores.

By far the highest-scoring pilots were various Germans. The highest-scoring of all was Erich Hartmann with 352, while tens of others claimed more than 100. These high totals reflected the fact that the Germans did not rotate top pilots out of combat to other

duties as often as other air forces. They were also mostly scored in the earlier years on the Eastern Front where enemy aircraft and pilots were relatively poor. One curiosity of the air fighting on the Eastern Front was that it was one of the few combat functions performed by women, though only on the Soviet side – several women became air aces.

Below: David McCampbell was the top US Navy ace of the war. He was eventually credited with 34 victories.

Medium Bombers, 1939–41

Whether intended to support ground campaigns or perform longer-range strategic attacks, early-war bombers struggled to achieve a good balance between the conflicting demands of speed, bomb load, range and defensive armament.

There is no exact definition of when an aircraft becomes a bomber rather than a close-support or ground-attack machine, but the "medium bombers" included here are the twin- or three-engined designs used by all air forces of the time for slightly or substantially longer-range missions.

Pre-war air forces almost all believed that formations of bombers each carrying as few as three machine-guns could defend themselves against enemy fighters and go on to bomb their targets accurately by day or by night. Experience would show that these claims were untrue, other than in very exceptional circumstances.

THE BLITZKRIEG ERA
Germany's Luftwaffe seemed to have the most powerful bomber force of the early-war years.

Above: He 111s in the Battle of Britain. Over 7,000 had been built by the time production ended in 1944.

This included three major types. Both the Dornier (Do) 17 and the Heinkel (He) 111 made their combat debuts during the Spanish Civil War, where their speed and the weakness of the opposition made them seem practically invulnerable. This was not confirmed in the Battle of Britain where their weak defensive armament and their modest bomb loads proved more relevant. The third type, the slightly later Junkers 88 (and the upgraded Do 217), were both more capable aircraft.

The contemporary British designs also had their own shortcomings. The Bristol Blenheim Mark 4 had a decent top speed of 428kph (266mph), for example, but only carried 455kg (1,000lb) of bombs. Neither the Blenheim nor its bigger stablemates were well-protected, though some of the larger aircraft included a British innovation of the mid-1930s – the power-operated gun turret. Least satisfactory of all was the Handley Page Hampden, which lost heavily in early daylight

Below: Savoia-Marchetti 79 Sparviero bombers. These were used for torpedo and bomb attacks.

operations and also lacked the range for night strategic bombing. The bigger Armstrong Whitworth Whitley carried a more substantial bomb load (up to 3,175kg/7,000lb) but it was no longer in front-line combat use by late 1943. The Vickers Wellington was much better. Its unusual web-like internal structure gave it enormous strength to go with a reasonable bomb load and speed.

Despite their defeats in 1939–40, various other air forces had aircraft of some potential, though these were seldom available in worthwhile numbers. Poland's PZL P37 was fast and had a good combination of range and bomb load, but the few in service were quickly overwhelmed. France's Farman F223 and Lioré et Olivier 45 both had impressive performance figures and fought well against the odds in 1940.

Various American designs also saw action with British or French forces before December 1941. The most important of these was the Douglas A-20, which was variously known as the Boston and Havoc and was used additionally in significant numbers by the Soviets.

THE MEDITERRANEAN

Italian designs in service in 1940 were essentially the same as those previously used in Abyssinia and Spain. They had been of good quality then, but Italy lacked the resources to develop replacements while also fighting these campaigns. The three-engined Savoia-Marchetti 79 Sparviero and the Fiat BR20 Cicogna were both in this category, though the Cant Z1007 Alcione was better.

DOUGLAS A-20B HAVOC

First used by France in 1940, the Havoc later served with the RAF and USAAF in the attack and night-fighter roles. In all some 9,500 were built up to 1944. The later A-20G variant was very heavily armed.

SPEED: 570kph (355mph)
RANGE: 1,770km (1,100 miles)
CREW: 4
ENGINES: 2 x Wright R-2600 Cyclone radials; 1,600hp each
ARMAMENT: 680kg (1,500lb) bombs; 3 x 0.5in (12.7mm) + 1 x 0.3in (7.62mm) MG

A number of American types also appeared in British service in the Mediterranean, notably the Martin A-22 Maryland and its development, the A-30 Baltimore. Neither saw combat later with the USAAF.

THE FAR EAST

The Japanese Army and Navy both had forces of land-based bombers. Designs that had seen some success in China during the 1930s continued service into the early stages of the Pacific War where they soon proved vulnerable to Allied fighters. These older types included the Mitsubishi Ki-30 "Ann" and the Kawasaki Ki-32 "Mary".

The Mitsubishi Ki-21 "Sally" was a later 1930s' Army design, broadly comparable to Western contemporaries, which included improved defensive armament in later versions. The Navy's Mitsubishi G3M "Nell" and the G4M "Betty" both had long range, but the G4M in particular was poorly protected.

HANDLEY PAGE HAMPDEN

The Hampden came into service in 1938 but was disappointing. Range with maximum bomb load was rather limited and defensive armament was poor. It left the Bomber Command service in 1942. About 700 of the 1,400 built were lost on operations.

SPEED: 410kph (255mph)
RANGE: 1,900km (1,200 miles)
CREW: 4
ENGINES: 2 x Bristol Pegasus XVIII; 980hp each
ARMAMENT: 1,800kg (4,000lb) bombs; 6 x 0.303in (7.7mm) machine-guns

Ground-attack Aircraft

Attack operations close to the front line were probably the most effective uses made of air power during the war. The Stuka symbolized Germany's early-war success and the Allied riposte was led by the Shturmovik, Typhoon and Thunderbolt.

In 1939 only the German and Soviet air forces laid any stress on the ground-attack mission. Germany's close integration of land and air power in the Blitzkrieg campaigns of 1939–41 proved that such operations could be very effective indeed. Britain and the USA would develop this capability in the course of the war.

Germany's Junkers 87 Stuka dive-bomber in effect became the definitive image of Blitzkrieg and was very much feared by opposing forces. In fact it was slow and poorly protected, as was shown when it first faced serious opposition during the Battle of Britain. However, it continued to serve successfully in the early Eastern Front battles – and the Ju-87G model, available from 1943, was fitted with a pair of 3.7cm (1.46in) cannon for the tank-busting role. It served very effectively in this mission, most notably in the hands of Hans-Ulrich Rudel, an ace pilot credited with destroying over 500 Soviet tanks.

Other German ground-attack types included versions of the Focke-Wulf (Fw) 190 fighter and the Fw 189, which was also used for reconnaissance. The Henschel 129 also served in small numbers, with armament including a 7.5cm (2.95in) gun.

THE RED AIR FORCE

By 1945 the Soviets had the world's most powerful tactical-support air force, created out of the ruins left by Germany's onslaught in 1941. Although the Soviet leaders had decided to concentrate on tactical aviation shortly before the war, their aircraft designs and training had not caught up with this change when Operation Barbarossa began.

There were various obsolete fighters in service in the attack role, including the biplane

Below: Ground crew bombing up a Typhoon fighter-bomber. It carries the "D-Day stripes" used in 1944–5.

P-47D THUNDERBOLT

The Republic P-47D Thunderbolt was particularly large and heavy for a WWII fighter, but its ample power meant that it could carry a heavy attack load. P-47D pilots claimed the destruction of tens of thousands of German tanks and trucks in Europe in 1944–5.

CREW: 1
ENGINE: Pratt & Whitney R2800 radial, 2,535hp
SPEED: 697kph (433mph)
ARMAMENT: 8 x 0.5in (12.7mm) machine-guns + 10 x 5in (127mm) rockets and/or up to 1,130kg (2,500lb) bombs

Above: A Ju-87G Stuka armed with 3.7cm (1.46in) anti-tank cannon.

Ilyushin (Il) 153 and the more modern Sukhoi 2. Just entering service was something much better – the Il-2 Bronirovanni Shturmovik (the "Armoured Attacker"), which eventually would become the most-produced military aircraft ever.

The Shturmovik was in effect a flying tank, with substantial armour protection for the crew compartment and other vital parts. It had powerful cannon and machine-gun armament (varying between models), backed by a substantial load of rockets and bombs. Formations of Shturmoviks would often circle round a German position or tank unit, making repeated attacks until their target had been smashed, a tactic called the "Circle of Death". In Soviet eyes it was the most important aircraft of the war.

Secondary, but still produced in substantial numbers (over 11,000), was the Petlyakov 2. This twin-engined design had

been conceived as a high-altitude fighter but was converted to the attack role. It was robust and fast and could carry 3 tonnes of bombs.

THE WESTERN ALLIES

In the absence of appropriate aircraft, Anglo-French ground-attack operations in 1940 were disastrous. Subsequently Britain began using versions of the Hurricane and P-40 Kittyhawk fighters in the role. These could carry a useful bomb load and had effective cannon and machine-gun armament – that included a pair of 40mm (1.58in) guns in one Hurricane variant) – but were lacking in performance when so equipped.

Fighter-bomber versions of the Bristol Beaufighter and De Havilland Mosquito were also employed, with some success. Both these large and powerful aircraft could carry formidable weapons loads but accuracy in attack remained uncertain.

From 1943 both British and US attack aircraft began using rockets. Although these lacked

IL-2M SHTURMOVIK

The prototype Shturmovik first flew in 1939 and a few were in service in 1941. Initial models were single-seaters but most production was of the two-seat Il-2M and -2M3 versions, which had various other improvements, too. Further changes led to the Il-10, which saw some action in 1945.

CREW: 2
ENGINE: Mikulin AM-38 in-line, 1,680hp
SPEED: 414kph (257mph)
ARMAMENT: 2 x 23mm (0.91in) cannon, 1 x 12.7mm (0.5in), 2 x 7.62mm (0.3in) machine-guns + 4 x RS82 or RS132 rockets and/or up to 600kg (1,320lb) bombs

the pinpoint accuracy to knock out a tank, they had the ability to swamp a larger or less well-protected target with fire.

Their best-known use was when fitted to aircraft like Britain's Hawker Typhoon and the USA's Republic P-47 Thunderbolt. Both of these were originally pure fighter designs (the Thunderbolt a successful one, the Typhoon less so), which had the power and durability to blossom in the attack role. They played a vital part in the Anglo-American victory in Europe in 1944–5.

Night Fighters

During WWII radar developments gradually stripped away the cover of darkness from night air operations. Starting with the Blitz in 1940–1, night fighters took an increasing toll of attacking and defending aircraft in a bitter struggle for supremacy.

No night-fighter aircraft existed anywhere at the beginning of WWII; night air defence relied on an inadequate combination of searchlights and anti-aircraft guns. However, by the later stages of the 1940–1 Blitz, Britain had introduced the first effective night fighters, directed by ground radar to a position near the target aircraft and then closing in to attack, using their own airborne radar equipment. Most night fighting would follow this pattern for the remainder of the war, though the radars used grew in range and precision, and counter-measures to defeat them became more sophisticated.

BRITISH DESIGNS

The Bristol Beaufighter was the first successful night fighter; like most night fighters of the war, it was a two-seat, twin-engined design. Twin engines left the aircraft nose free for the radar equipment (and usually heavy guns as well) and gave the power necessary to over-come the drag often caused by bulky aerials; the second crew-man was the radar operator. The Beaufighter made its opera-tional debut in September 1940 and achieved its first success over the next month.

From 1941 it was joined and eventually replaced by a series of variants of the De Havilland Mosquito. This was fast and long-ranged and very heavily armed – commonly four 20mm (0.79in) cannon and four machine-guns – and equipped with successively improved models of radar. Late-war versions also carried Serrate equipment to home in on German night-fighter radar signals. By then night-intruder operations over enemy territory were the main mission for the Allied night-fighter force.

Since there was little like-lihood of night air attack on the USA and the US bomber forces operated by day, American night-fighter development was rather slower. Initially US night-fighter units used the Beaufighter and versions of the A-20 Havoc bomber, but they were converted from mid-1944 to the Northrop P-61 Black

---

NORTHROP P-61

The P-61 Black Widow first flew in 1942 and was first deployed on operations in June 1944, in both the Pacific and Europe. Some 740 were built in all. Some variants had only the nose-mounted cannon and two crew; others had a fully trainable turret with two or four machine-guns.

CREW: 2 or 3
ENGINES: 2 x Pratt & Whitney R-2800-65; 2,250hp each
SPEED: 589kph (366mph)
CEILING: 10,100m (33,100ft)
ARMAMENT: 4 x 20mm (0.79in) cannon + 4 x 0.5in (12.7mm) machine-guns

---

HEINKEL 219

Germany's chaotic air procure-ment system is illustrated by the He 219, only produced after significant private invest-ment by the manufacturer. Speed and altitude perform-ance were generally much better than earlier German types, but it compared poorly with the Mosquito or P-61.

CREW: 2
ENGINES: 2 x Daimler Benz 603
SPEED (A-7): 616kph (383mph)
RANGE: 1,540km (960 miles)
CEILING: 9,300m (30,500ft)
ARMAMENT: up to 4 x 3cm (1.18in) + 4 x 2cm (0.79in) cannon

Above: A German Ju 88 night fighter fitted with the clumsy aerial array of the Lichtenstein SN-2 radar.

Widow. This was the only purpose-built night fighter to see service with any nation during the war and had virtually identical performance characteristics and armament to the Mosquito.

The US Navy also used a number of Corsair and Hellcat single-seat, single-engined fighters at night, fitted with radar sets in the wings.

GERMANY'S REPLY

Since it faced the most sustained night-bombing attacks of the war, Germany naturally responded with significant night-fighter developments, though these were hampered by the poor organization of German aircraft procurement and electronics research.

Early types included versions of the Messerschmitt (Me) Bf 110 fighter and Junkers (Ju) 88 bomber. Both could carry a heavy armament, including the *Schräge Musik* ("Jazz Music") upward-firing cannon used from the blind spot underneath a target aircraft. However, performance suffered because of the drag from the large aerials required by the German Lichtenstein radar sets.

A variety of other models were also used, including the Me 210 and 410, and the Ju 188 and 388. The most capable of all, but produced in limited numbers (fewer than 300), was the Heinkel 219, in service from the summer of 1943.

Germany also made extensive use of unmodified single-engined day fighters in the night-fighter role. Since the British night bombers operated in concentrated streams, a fighter directed to the stream had a reasonable chance of acquiring a target visually, especially close to the bombing target when flares and ground fires gave

extra illumination. This *Wilde Sau* ("Wild Boar") tactic was introduced initially when British counter-measures blinded the German radar control system for a time in mid-1943. This was used with success for the remainder of the war.

Japan had a limited night-fighter force, in part because of the lack of effective Japanese radar equipment. The Navy's Nakajima J1N "Irving" had a small number of successes over the Home Islands and elsewhere, and the Army's Kawasaki Ki-102 "Randy" was potentially a capable aircraft but only appeared in modest numbers.

BRISTOL BEAUFIGHTER

Developed from the Beaufort torpedo bomber, the Beaufighter first flew in July 1939. It was used as a radar-equipped night fighter from the autumn of 1940 but was gradually replaced in this role by the Mosquito. Torpedo-bomber and strike variants saw extensive use to the end of the war.

CREW: 2
ENGINES: 2 x Bristol Hercules III; 1,400hp each
SPEED: 540kph (335mph)
RANGE: 2,400km (1,500 miles)
CEILING: 8,800m (28,900ft)
ARMAMENT: 4 x 20mm (0.79in) cannon

Heavy Bombers

The four-engined heavy bombers of the British and US air forces were among the most potent weapons of the war. They combined high-tech electronic equipment with the brute power to deliver tonnes of bombs deep inside an enemy country.

From the later years of WWI airforce officers in various countries had argued that, if suitably equipped and expanded, their services could win a war by bombing attacks on the industries and people of an enemy homeland. Such attacks were called strategic bombing (as distinct from tactical operations near a land battle front).

In WWII Britain and the USA were the only countries to equip themselves for such operations and try to win the war by carrying them out. At the heart of strategic bombing campaigns were the various four-engined bombers described here.

The first aircraft of this type to enter service was the Boeing B-17 Flying Fortress, first flown

in 1935 and in series production from 1939. This had impressive performance but, with only five hand-trained machine-guns and lacking self-sealing fuel tanks and adequate armour protection for the crew, early marks hardly lived up to their name. Significant improvements came

Above: A pair of B-24 Liberators escorted by P-40 fighters on a mission in the north Pacific in 1944.

with the B-17E version, in use from 1942; the final B-17G carried 13 defensive guns.

At first sight the B-17's near contemporary, the Consolidated B-24 Liberator (first flown in 1939), was superior. It was faster, and had a better range, with the same bomb load and similar defensive armament. However, in action it was found to be less suited to the tight formation flying at high altitude needed for operations over Germany. Like the B-17 it went through various marks before reaching its best defended final version, the B-24J.

DAY BOMBING

Throughout the war in Europe US tactics were to carry out strategic bombing raids by day in the hope of bombing with great accuracy. This dictated the heavy defensive armament fitted to the B-17 and B-24 and

---

BOEING B-17G FLYING FORTRESS

The B-17G was the definitive version of this aircraft. About two-thirds of the 12,700 B-17s were of this model. Improvements on the original included a lengthened fuselage, larger tail, and chin and tail turrets.

SPEED: 462kph (287mph)
ENGINES: 4 x Wright Cyclone R1820 radials; 1,500hp each
RANGE: 3,200km (2,000 miles)
ARMAMENT: 13 x 0.5in (12.7mm) machine-guns; typically 2,000kg (4,400lb) bombs

PIAGGIO P.108B

Italy's P.108B was one of the few heavy bombers outside the UK and US forces to see action. The P.108B was a powerful and effective machine with various advanced features, including remotely controlled gun turrets.

SPEED: 430kph (267mph)
ENGINES: 4 x Piaggio PXII RC35 radials; 1,500hp each
RANGE: 3,540km (2,200 miles)
ARMAMENT: 6 x 12.7mm (0.5in) + 2 x 7.7mm (0.303in) machine-guns; 3,500kg (7,700lb) bombs

also resulted in their having relatively modest bomb loads of some 2.5 tonnes. In the event bombing accuracy in cloudy European conditions was much less than in Stateside trials and, until the advent of long-range escort fighters in 1944, bomber losses were extremely heavy.

BRITISH TACTICS

Britain's RAF began the war equally convinced that its bombers could fight their way to their targets in daylight. However, bitter experience soon proved otherwise and Bomber Command switched to night raids on Germany.

Though twin-engined types featured in these attacks into 1943, four-engined designs to replace these entered service from early 1941. Relying on the cover of darkness, all had weaker defensive armament than the US types but much greater bomb loads. Bombing accuracy was very poor in the early stages of the campaign, but it improved substantially later as electronic aids to navigation were introduced and improved.

The first type, the Short Stirling, only saw front-line use until 1943 – its low service ceiling made it unacceptably vulnerable. The Handley Page Halifax, which came next, was a significant improvement, especially the later Mark 3 type, and served to the end of the war. Undoubtedly the best British heavy bomber of the war, however, was the Avro Lancaster, in squadron service from early 1942. Over 7,000 of this tough and reliable aircraft were built.

Taking the war to Japan demanded a longer-range aircraft than those deployed in Europe, and design work on what became the Boeing B-29 Superfortress began before the war. The prototype first flew in 1942 but, between then and its combat debut in mid-1944, there were many problems and modifications to be addressed. This was largely because, in addition to its great size, it was an extremely complex and technologically advanced aircraft. However, with the development of bases in the Mariana Islands later in 1944, it was able to begin attacks on Japan, culminating in the nuclear missions that finally ended the war.

Below: A flight of Short Stirling bombers during training in 1942. The Stirling was the least effective of the three British four-engined designs.

Medium Bombers, 1942–5

By the end of the war the Allied air forces had long since gained total air superiority and this was nowhere better seen than in the operations of the thousands of Anglo-American medium bombers over Europe and in the Pacific.

The British and American medium bombers of 1942–5 include some of the most famous aircraft of the era. However, comparable Axis aircraft of the time remain little known. This is no coincidence. It simply reflects the failure of the Germans and Japanese to respond effectively to the Allied challenge in the air. (The Soviets also had few medium or heavy bombers but this derived from their total concentration on ground-attack aircraft and fighters, not a lack of effective air power.)

THE WOODEN WONDER

Britain only produced one aircraft in this class, but it was one of the best: the De Havilland

Below: A Mitsubishi Ki-67 *Hiryu* ("Flying Dragon") bomber, known to the Allies as "Peggy". In service from late 1944, the Ki-67 was fast (537kph/334mph) and better armed than previous Japanese bombers.

Mosquito. Almost 7,000 were built during the war, including photo-reconnaissance, ground-attack and night-fighter variants, as well as bombers.

All were fast and could carry a substantial load of bombs, guns or other equipment – and were made mainly of wood! In service with RAF Bomber Command, Mosquitos supported the main heavy-bomber force by flying diversionary raids and marking targets.

MAIN US TYPES

US medium-bomber aircraft included the Douglas A-20 Havoc/Boston, in service from early in the war, the North American B-25 Mitchell, Martin B-26 Marauder and Douglas A-26 Invader. A-designation aircraft were supposedly optimized for the (ground-) attack role, while the B-types were for the somewhat different medium-bomber mission. In practice

MOSQUITO B MARK 16

Mosquito bombers could carry a 4,000lb bomb (as shown) or a range of flares and target markers. Over 1,200 of the Mark 16 were built, the most numerous bomber version.

SPEED: 668kph (415mph)
RANGE: 2,400km (1,500 miles)
CREW: 2
ENGINES: 2 x Rolls-Royce Merlin 76/77; 1,710hp each
ARMAMENT: 1,800kg (4,000lb) bombs or flares; no guns

Right: A B-25H Mitchell in flight. This was one of the attack variants of the Mitchell, with a solid nose rather than a glazed bombardier's position. It carried eight forward-firing machine-guns and a 75mm cannon.

there was much overlap. The B-25 served throughout US involvement in the war and, like all the American aircraft mentioned above, was supplied in quantity to various Allies under Lend-Lease. Almost 10,000 were produced, in many variants that included several for the attack role, with up to 12 nose-mounted machine-guns and a 75mm (2.95in) cannon. Pure bomber versions could carry up to 2,700kg (6,000lb) of bombs.

There was little to choose between the B-25 and B-26 in performance or service career, though most of the 4,700 B-26s built for the USAAF were sent to Europe. The B-26 eventually had the lowest loss rate of any major USAAF combat aircraft, but when it was first introduced there were numerous accidents, avoided later by aircraft modifications and better pilot training.

Both the B-25 and B-26 saw combat from 1942, but the A-26 did not begin operations until mid-1944; over 1,000 were in use by 1945 and the type continued to serve for many years after the war. It carried similar armament to the Mitchell and Marauder but had only a three-man crew: pilot, navigator/bombardier and air gunner, who operated remotely controlled dorsal and ventral turrets

GERMANY AND JAPAN

In the mid war years German aircraft production planning was virtually non-existent, with a great deal of effort being wasted on minor upgrades of already obsolescent types and the development of numerous prototype designs. When this was set right in 1944-5, far too late, bomber production had to be virtually abandoned in favour of fighters. Thus the Dornier 217K, probably Germany's best bomber of the war, was taken out of production in late 1943.

One notable type that was introduced into service was the Heinkel 177. This unusual design appeared to be twin-engined but actually had a pair of engines in each wing to drive the single propellers. It had reasonable performance figures overall, but early examples in particular were very prone to disastrous engine fires.

Japan's aircraft industry never had the strength to compete with its enemies. Later-war bomber types included the Yokosuka P1Y "Frances", the Nakajima Ki-49 "Helen" and the Mitsubishi Ki 67 "Peggy". Fewer than 1,000 of each bomber were made.

MARTIN B-26 MARAUDER

First flown in 1940, the B-26 saw its first combat in the South Pacific in 1942. Most served in Europe, however. Some 5,300 were built in all and they were used by all the US services and various British Empire air forces.

SPEED: 462kph (287mph)
RANGE: 1,850km (1,150 miles)
CREW: 7
ENGINES: 2 x Pratt & Whitney R2800; 1,900hp each
ARMAMENT: 1,800kg (4,000lb) bombs; 12 x machine-guns

Fighters, 1943–5

By late 1944, thanks to the British, American and Soviet fighter forces and their range of superb aircraft, Allied heavy bombers ranged freely over Germany and Japan and ground-attack aircraft dominated the Axis land forces on all fronts.

From mid-1943 Allied air superiority over every battle-front was clear, and during 1944 was extended to cover both the German and the Japanese homelands by day and by night. It was the Allied fighters that made this happen. Although Germany and Japan both continued to field highly effective piston-engined fighters, overall the Allies had a qualitative advantage (other than over Germany's jets) to add to their enormous numerical superiority.

ALLIED DESIGNS

The USAAF was the world's strongest air force in 1944–5 and had the fighters to match. The main types were the North American P-51 Mustang and the Republic P-47 Thunderbolt, both dating from 1940–1, although the earlier P-38 Lightning also remained in use.

The P-47 seemed the more promising design initially. It was based around a particularly large and powerful radial engine, which gave it an impressive rate of climb and dive despite its imposing size and weight. The P-47D version was the most built subtype of any fighter ever, with over 12,000 made.

After an unpromising start the P-51 Mustang developed into the aircraft that did more than any other to win the air war over western Europe. Fitted with the initial Allison engine, the Mustang had disappointing flight performance, especially at

P-51D MUSTANG

The P-51D is regarded as the definitive wartime version of the Mustang. Like its B and C model predecessors, it was fitted with an American-built Packard Merlin engine but had two extra machine-guns and a "bubble" cockpit canopy for improved pilot visibility. Over 8,000 P-51Ds and some 16,000 of all P-51 marks were built.

SPEED: 703kph (437mph)
RANGE: 2,655km (1,650 miles), with drop tanks
CREW: 1
ENGINE: Packard Merlin V-1650; 1,695hp
ARMAMENT: 6 x 0.5in (12.7mm) machine-guns

Left: Late-war P-47 Thunderbolts were fitted with a "bubble" cockpit canopy to improve pilot visibility.

altitude; but in 1942 a version with a Rolls-Royce Merlin engine was tested and the Mustang was transformed. Fitted with drop tanks for additional fuel, the new aircraft had the range to escort bombers from England to Berlin and beyond and was superior to almost all Luftwaffe fighters when it got there, a combination of range and performance previously thought to be impossible.

In the final stages of the war many British fighter units continued to use the Spitfire Mark 9, introduced in 1942. This was joined by variants, notably the Mark 14, in which the Merlin engine was replaced by a more powerful Rolls-Royce Griffon. These gave nothing away to contemporaries in speed and manoeuvrability but, like earlier Spitfires, lacked range.

Completing the formidable Allied line-up was a range of impressive Soviet designs, the best of which came from the Yakovlev and Lavochkin design bureaux. The Yak-9, introduced in 1942, was an effective upgrade of the earlier Yak-7, with a more powerful engine and better armament fit. Its upgrade to the 9U version in 1944 was even more impressive. The ultimate Yak fighter of the war, also introduced in 1944, was the confusingly designated Yak-3.

Above: A formation of Yak-9D escort fighters in flight. Over 16,500 Yak-9 fighters were built.

This was an extremely fast and manoeuvrable design, probably the best fighter of the war on the Eastern Front. The La-5 and La-7, developed from the previous LaGG designs, were both also very effective if not quite the equals of the Yak types.

AXIS REPLIES

Germany's Focke-Wulf 190 had outclassed the RAF's Spitfires when introduced in 1941. Versions of this design and later marks of the Messerschmitt Bf 109 remained the principal German fighters until the end of the war. By 1944 the Bf 109 and the radial-engined versions of the Fw 190 struggled to compete with the best Allied aircraft. The Fw 190D, fitted with an in-line engine and available from late 1944, was faster and more formidable.

In the Pacific War Japan's aircraft industry also failed to keep up with new designs. As a token

of this, the Kawasaki Ki-61 "Tony" (one of the most significant later-war Japanese fighters) was only one of several Japanese aircraft relying on licence-built versions of German engines. The best Japanese Army fighter of the war was the Nakajima Ki-84 "Frank", in service from April 1944.

Below: A Griffon-engined Spitfire Mark 14 in flight. The Mark 14 had a top speed of 721kph (448mph).

FOCKE-WULF 190

Over 20,000 Fw 190s were built in numerous variants, including the radically different D model and successors with an in-line rather than a radial engine. The Fw 190 served as a fighter, including some with heavy armour and armament for the bomber-attack role, and as a fighter-bomber.

SPECIFICATION: Fw 190A-3
SPEED: 640kph (398mph)
RANGE: 800km (500 miles)
CREW: 1
ENGINE: BMW 801 D-2; 1,730hp
ARMAMENT: 2 x 20mm (0.79in) cannon + 2 x 7.92mm (0.312in) machine-guns

Aircraft Ordnance and Electronics

Air attacks were meaningless without effective weapons and systems to guide aircraft to their targets. Bombs, rockets, radar, navigation aids and equipment to jam or home in on enemy transmissions all saw substantial development during the war.

It is well known that WWII saw much behind-the-scenes innovation in radar and other aspects of aircraft electronics, but developments in seemingly mundane fields like bomb design were also significant.

BOMBS AND ROCKETS

Many different bombs were used, from 1.8kg (4lb) incendiaries, dropped by the millions, to the RAF's 9,980kg (22,000lb) Grand Slam of which 41 were used in 1945. By the later stages of the war a typical British heavy-bomber load for an attack on a German city would include a single "cookie" (a large, high-capacity, high-explosive bomb) to blast buildings open, as well as a range of incendiaries to set them on fire. In the 1945 US attacks on Japanese cities incendiary bombs were the principal types used. By 1945 ground-attack and anti-shipping aircraft in US, British and Soviet service were also using un-guided air-to-ground rockets as a major part of their armoury.

Although most bombs were "dumb" free-fall weapons, various guided and powered bombs

Above: A *Mistel* composite aircraft. The pair would be flown to the target by the fighter pilot who would then release the crewless but explosive-filled bomber to complete the attack. *Mistel* aircraft achieved little success.

were developed. German types included the rocket-powered Hs 293 and the free-fall Fritz-X; the American Azon type was similar to the Fritz-X. All were radio-controlled from the dropping aircraft, which had to keep the bomb and the target in sight throughout, always tricky and often dangerous. The American Bat type was potentially more capable because it included its

own radar set, which it used to home in on its target. German successes included the sinking of the Italian battleship *Roma* by a Fritz-X in September 1943.

ELECTRONIC WARFARE

All major nations had some degree of radar capability in 1939, but Britain, the USA and Germany were the only ones to make substantial developments in this field. The accuracy of radar sets increased substantially during the war, as did the variety of methods to fool them and in turn the devices made to overcome these.

The most used anti-radar device was strips of metal foil dropped from an aircraft to give a mass of false radar returns on enemy screens – provided the strips were cut to the correct size according to the radar wavelength. This was first used by

Left: A Messerschmitt 110 night fighter fitted with Lichtenstein radar.

Right: Ground crewmen loading a 4,000lb (1,815kg) High Capacity bomb into a Lancaster.

British forces in July 1943 and in updated forms provided significant protection to British and American aircraft over Germany and Japan to the end of the war.

The Luftwaffe was the only air force in 1939 to appreciate the difficulty of finding bombing targets by night or in bad weather and had various radio-beam systems (Knickebein, X-Gerät and Y-Gerät) in service to achieve this. These were used with some success during the Blitz in 1940–1, but once British scientists had worked out how they operated, the systems were relatively easy to jam.

The British Gee, introduced in 1942, worked on a similar triangulation principle and was also jammed after a few months' use. The later Oboe used radar to measure the range between the aircraft and various ground stations. A disadvantage of all these was that their range was limited by the curvature of the Earth to about 450km (280 miles).

Slightly later still was the H2S system (used by American forces as H2X and in an improved APS-20 form), a ground-mapping radar operated by the aircraft independently of any ground station. This worked best when the ground below had distinctive features like a river or coastline. With devices like these, the RAF heavy-bomber force of 1944–5 was able to attack at least as accurately at night as the American bomber groups by day.

All such devices brought a disadvantage, however. The enemy could use any radio or radar transmitter in an aircraft to home in on it. Late-war British Mosquito night fighters, for example, had effective equipment called Perfectos and Serrate to do just this to their German counterparts.

Right: An Avro Lancaster in flight with the distinctive bulge of its H2S ground-mapping radar clearly visible under the rear fuselage.

Jet Aircraft

Although the piston-engined aircraft in service in 1944–5 were vastly superior to those used at the start of the war, they were clearly outclassed by the new turbojet types, even though all of these had reliability issues and other problems.

Although the power of air-craft piston engines was improved very substantially during the course of WWII, it was also clear that there was more potential for the future in rocket and turbojet propulsion. All the major combatants were working on such designs by 1945, but only Germany and Britain used jet aircraft in combat before the end of the war; the USA had jets in service but not yet deployed on operations.

FIRST JETS

The first workable jet engines were made in 1937 in separate research programmes in Britain and Germany. At that stage the British design by Frank Whittle was more advanced, but Heinz von Ohain's engine was the first to fly, in the Heinkel (He) 178 in 1939. Whittle's Gloster E.28/39 first flew in 1941. Neither of these was intended as a combat aircraft, but two

GLOSTER METEOR F 1

The Gloster Meteor was the first operational Allied jet. The illustrated example, an F 1, is in flight over Kent in August 1944, days after the type's combat debut. The later F 3 had better Derwent engines and improved aerodynamics.

SPEED: 670kph (417mph)
RANGE: 880km (550 miles)
CREW: 1
ENGINES: 2 x Rolls-Royce W2B Welland turbojets
ARMAMENT: 4 x 20mm (0.79in) cannon

designs which were took to the air in 1941–2: the Messer-schmitt (Me) 163 and Me 262.

The Me 163 came from a completely different line of development. With an entire-ly unconventional arrowhead shape and powered by a Walther rocket engine, it could reach an incredible 960kph (596mph). Disadvantages were that it only carried fuel for about ten min-utes of flight; that the fuel itself was dangerously prone to explo-sion; and that after its brief flight the aircraft had to glide back to base and land using skids, not a proper under-carriage. It began operations in mid-1944 and achieved a few successes against Allied bombers, but accidents and other problems were common.

The turbojet and Me 262 offered better prospects, though it took two years from the type's first flight in July 1942 for it to reach combat. This was mainly caused by engine and other faults, but Hitler's order that it was to be adapted as a fast bomber certainly did not help.

Although perhaps 1,400 were built, far fewer reached the squadrons and they suffered fuel shortages and other prob-lems. They could outfly any Allied aircraft and were well-armed for bomber interception, but many were shot down while

Left: The Me 163 rocket fighter was stunningly fast but probably shot down fewer than 20 Allied aircraft.

ARADO 234

The Arado 234 first flew in June 1943. Early production versions, designated Ar 234B (see specification below), had two Junkers engines. The illustrated example is a 234C, with four BMW 003A engines, which was significantly faster but was still in prototype form when the war ended.

SPEED: 742kph (461mph)
RANGE: 1,100km (680 miles) with bomb load
CREW: 1
ENGINES: 2 x Junkers Jumo 004B-1 turbojets
ARMAMENT: 1,500kg (3,300lb) bombs; usually no guns

landing or taking off from their bases when they were slow-moving and vulnerable.

Two more German jets were built and made operational but saw little combat. Over 200 Arado 234 bombers were produced in 1944–5 but saw only scattered action, notably against the Rhine Bridge at Remagen.

Some 50 of a simplified fighter type, the He 162 Volksjäger (or "People's Fighter") were built in the final months of the war. This design was meant to be suitable for operation by inexperienced pilots, but by the time it was available there was little fuel to be found. It probably flew a handful of combat missions in April 1945.

ALLIED TYPES

On the Allied side the American Bell P-59 Airacomet first flew in October 1942 but met repeated problems and was never taken into operational service. Two more US designs, the Lockheed P-80 and the Ryan FR-1 (this type having both a piston and a jet engine fitted), were being deployed when Japan surrendered but did not see combat.

Britain's Gloster Meteor flew in 1943 and came into operational use in July 1944. Initially F 1 models were employed in the home-defence role, operating against V-1 flying bombs, but a few much improved F 3s were deployed to bases on the Continent in 1945. Like the other early jets, it suffered from many teething problems and successive production batches showed numerous minor improvements to address these.

Right: A bomb-armed Me 262. Hitler insisted that the type should be developed as a fast bomber.

Transport Aircraft and Gliders

Air supply operations on an entirely new scale were possible in WWII, in Burma and China and many other places. Mass airborne operations also began, using aircraft and gliders to bring thousands of troops suddenly into action.

World War II was the first conflict in which air transport played a significant role. It was also the first in which airborne warfare, using parachute and glider-borne troops, was employed in major battles.

TRANSPORT AIRCRAFT

The best-known transport aircraft of the early-war years was Germany's Junkers 52. Dating back to the early 1930s and with an unusual three-engined configuration, the Ju 52 had modest flight performance and could carry 18 fully armed troops. It dropped paratroops and towed gliders in Germany's early campaigns, but was less successful as a cargo carrier ferrying supplies to the surrounded Sixth Army at Stalingrad.

Below: A Ju 52 on a Russian airfield, 1941–2. Ju 52s supplied many surrounded troops that winter but failed to repeat the feat in 1942–3.

Above: A flight of Horsa gliders being towed aloft (by converted Whitley bombers) in training in 1943.

Germany also had the huge six-engined Messerschmitt 323, converted from a glider. It could carry an unequalled 21 tonnes of cargo but was very slow and vulnerable to fighter attack.

Britain depended mainly on American designs for its transport aircraft but did employ some converted heavy bombers in the role. Whitleys, Stirlings and Halifaxes all towed gliders and dropped paratroops; Avro York conversions of the Lancaster could carry 10 tonnes of cargo. The Armstrong Whitworth Albemarle, originally intended as a bomber, saw most service as a glider tug.

The USA made far more use of transport aircraft than any other nation, as well as supplying

many of these to all the Allies. The oldest design, based on the Douglas DC-3 airliner of the mid-1930s, served as the C-47 Skytrain (or Dakota in British service). Over 10,000 were made and served in all transport roles in all theatres (when configured to carry paratroops they were officially known as C-53 Skytroopers).

Serving mainly against Japan was a second twin-engined design, the Curtiss C-46 Commando. Though it was faster and could carry much

C-54 SKYMASTER

The C-54 was developed from the pre-war Douglas DC-4 airliner, first flown in 1938. The first C-54 entered service in 1942 and in all 1,170 were built. It also served with the US Navy as the R5D and with various Allied countries. A number of C-54s were used for VIP transport, including one by President Roosevelt.

ENGINES: 4 x 1,450hp Pratt & Whitney R-2000 Cyclone radials
CRUISING SPEED: 310kph (190mph)
RANGE: 6,400km (4,000 miles)
CREW: 4
CAPACITY: 50 passengers or equivalent cargo

more cargo than the C-47, only about 3,300 were made. Most served on the notoriously demanding "Over the Hump" supply route to China. Finally, the US had the four-engined C-54 Skymaster, based on the pre-war Douglas DC-4 airliner. This could carry up to 50 personnel or an equivalent cargo and mainly operated to and from bases in the USA.

GLIDERS

Even if at first glance they might seem dangerously unsuited to military uses, gliders had valuable attributes that helped them see much effective war service. They could carry significant numbers of troops into action and land each planeload in a concentrated group (paratroops might be scattered far and wide); they flew silently and could land very accurately beside, or even on top of, an objective (as was done by the Germans at Eben Emael in 1940 and by various British units on D-Day); and the troops they carried did not need to be carefully selected or given specialized parachute training.

Above: US paratroops embark in a C-53 Skytrooper. A typical load was 15–18 troops and their equipment.

Countries using significant numbers of gliders were Britain, Germany and the USA.

Germany's main glider was the DFS 230. It could carry ten men, including the pilot. (Glider pilots in all nations were usually expected to get out and fight after landing.) Larger types included the Gotha 242 and the Me 321 Gigant, parent design of the Me 323 described above. The Gigant needed three Me 110s or a specially adapted Heinkel 111 to tow it aloft, so it was not a success.

British gliders included the Airspeed Horsa, which could carry 30 men or an anti-tank gun or similar cargo, and the much larger General Aircraft Hamilcar, which could lift a light tank. The main American glider (over 12,000 built) was the CG-4A Waco, which could carry 15 men or an equivalent cargo. British and American gliders played a vital part in the invasions of Sicily and Normandy and other major airborne operations.

NAVAL WEAPONS

Although no new naval weapons were introduced during WWII, the existing armoury of guns, torpedoes and depth charges were given new accuracy and striking power from developments in control systems and detection equipment. This chapter features key weapons, such as battleships and submarines.

Image: The German battle-cruiser Scharnhorst pictured in 1939 in a harbour on the North German coast.

Heavy Cruisers

The heavy cruisers of World War II were the product of an intense arms race during the inter-war period. Japan built particularly large and powerful ships by flagrant violation of treaty limits; other navies strove to keep up.

Since battleship design was very tightly controlled by the Washington Naval Treaty and its successors, much inter-war competition between the leading navies came to be in cruiser construction, whether the heavy cruisers armed with 203mm (8in) guns covered here or lighter 152mm (6in) armed types.

In the inter-war period the "treaty limit" for cruisers was 10,000 tons standard displacement. Japan, Italy and later Germany all flagrantly breached this figure, but other nations generally kept fairly close to it. In fact, the limit of 10,000 tons/ 8in guns had been arrived at rather arbitrarily. It was actually very difficult to build ships to these figures that also had a reasonable balance of armour protection and engine power.

TREATY CRUISERS

Japan and Italy were the first to build "treaty" heavy cruisers, in the mid-1920s. Japan's *Furutaka* was a relatively modest design with six single 200mm (7.87in) guns, reasonable side armour and 33-knot speed, on an official displacement of 7,000 tons (actually about 2,000 more).

Italy's *Trento* and *Trieste* were equally fast with 8 x 203mm guns. However, although their true displacement was about 11,500 tons, they were still rather flimsily built. The four later Italian Zara-class ships were much better armoured and several knots slower.

Japan's successor ships to the *Furutaka* also substantially breached the treaty limits. The Myoko and Atago classes were all over 13,000 tons, carried 10 x 203mm guns and a heavy torpedo armament, with armour up to 120mm (4.72in) thick.

In comparison with these, British and American inter-war ships looked rather second-rate.

Left: The pocket battleship *Admiral Graf Spee* in mid-1939. The *Graf Spee* was scuttled in December 1939 after the Battle of the River Plate.

IJNS *FURUTAKA*

The *Furutaka* had a relatively brief combat career in WWII. After serving in various early battles, *Furutaka* was part of the successful Japanese force in the Battle of Savo Island off Guadalcanal but was sunk in the Cape Esperance engagement in October 1942.

SISTER SHIP: *Kako*
COMMISSIONED: 1926
DISPLACEMENT: 9,000 tons
SPEED: 33 knots
BELT ARMOUR: 76mm (3in) max.
ARMAMENT: 6 x 200mm (7.87in) + 4 x 119mm (4.7in) guns

Britain built a series of similar ships, collectively known as the County class. They all carried 8 x 8in guns on a displacement very close to 10,000 tons. They had very good range and sea-keeping qualities but had very little armour and a high silhouette, which made them rather vulnerable in action. Britain also built two smaller ships with 8in guns in the early 1930s – the *Exeter* and *York* – but like most

HMS *KENT*

HMS *Kent* was the nameship of the first group of seven County-class cruisers. *Kent* served in the Mediterranean initially but was damaged in 1940. *Kent* is seen below in 1941 after repairs, in service with the Home Fleet, its station for the rest of the war.

SISTER SHIPS: 6, inc. 2 Australian
COMMISSIONED: 1928
DISPLACEMENT: 10,000 tons
SPEED: 32 knots
BELT ARMOUR: 115mm (4.53in)
ARMAMENT: 8 x 8in (203mm)
+ 10 x 4in (102mm) guns

other navies did not build any more 8in heavy cruisers during the war.

Germany operated within a different set of restrictions, having to conform (until Hitler abrogated it) to the Versailles Treaty. In the late 1920s Germany was allowed to begin work on replacements for old coast-defence ships that had previously been permitted under Versailles.

The replacements were three *Panzerschiffe* (armoured ships), soon termed "pocket battleships" by British commentators, but better described as heavy cruisers, as they were eventually officially designated. They carried two triple 280mm (11in) turrets and could reach 26 knots, but significantly exceeded their announced 10,000-ton displacement (cheating that in fact pre-dated Hitler's regime). Supposedly, they had the gunpower to outmatch any cruiser and the speed to escape almost any battleship. However, these ships proved unsatisfactory, with slow-firing armament and unreliable engines. Three later German 203mm-armed cruisers were also built, again large and formidable vessels but troubled by weak engines.

AMERICAN DESIGNS

The US Navy built several classes of "treaty cruisers". First were two Salt Lake City ships with an unusual arrangement of a twin and triple turret fore and aft, with the triples superfiring over the twins; unsurprisingly, they were somewhat top-heavy.

Subsequent American classes changed to three triple 8in turrets, which proved to be a more sensible arrangement. As well as commissioning numerous 6in cruisers, US industrial power also saw the completion of more than a dozen Baltimore-class ships during the war. These kept the same main armament as earlier 8in vessels but increased displacement to 13,600 tons, to fit in the extra equipment that war experience showed to be necessary.

Below: The Astoria-class USS *Vincennes* in July 1942. It was sunk a few weeks later off Guadalcanal.

Anti-submarine Escort Ships

Ships designed for anti-submarine duties did not need to be large or fast or carry numerous guns. Instead the British and US fleets built hundreds of tough and enduring smaller ships, which took a huge toll of enemy submarine forces.

The main anti-submarine vessels in all navies were traditionally destroyers. However, these were expensive to build and their design emphasized speed and anti-ship armament, not endurance and anti-submarine weapons. In World War II, large numbers of smaller and usually slower ships were built, designed and equipped mainly or exclusively for anti-submarine work.

Above: The destroyer escort USS *Huse* and an escort carrier hunting for Atlantic U-boats in 1944.

JAPAN'S FAILURE

The major operators of ships in this category were the British and Americans (who supplied ships and designs to other Allied navies and also used each other's designs). The other navy with large ocean-going responsibilities, the Japanese, notably failed in anti-submarine operations, especially in defence of merchant ships. There were two reasons for this: first, both before and during the war the Japanese concentrated on offensive operations against enemy warships; and, second, they devoted little effort to developing radar and sonar equipment, crucial in the anti-submarine war. Some Japanese escorts had no underwater sensors as late as 1942, a year in which the Japanese Navy ordered the grand total of eight escort-type ships. By contrast the Royal Navy built around 600 escorts in its principal classes in the course of the war, while the US Navy produced many more.

Important British escort ship classes were: Black Swan sloops, Hunt escort destroyers, Loch and

---

HMS *LOCH FADA*

Seen here in April 1944 around the time of its commissioning, HMS *Loch Fada* was the first of the 28 Loch-class frigates. The design was a development of the previous River-class frigate, but it had much better anti-submarine weapons and sensors.

COMMISSIONED: 1944
DISPLACEMENT: 1,400 tons
CREW: 114
SPEED: 20 knots
ARMAMENT: 1 x 4in (102mm) + various light anti-aircraft guns; 2 x Squid anti-submarine mortars + depth charge rails and throwers

River frigates and Flower and Castle corvettes. The Hunts and Black Swans were built to standard navy specifications and were effectively smaller and slower destroyers. The Hunt class (86 built) were a little over 1,000 tons standard displacement and could make 27 knots with 4 or 6 x 4in (102mm) guns; some carried 3 torpedo tubes. Fewer Black Swan-class ships were built, similar in size and armament but with a lower top speed (20 knots), in exchange for longer endurance.

The other escort ship classes did not have a purely naval heritage but were designed to be suitable for building in yards without naval experience and to use mercantile engines. In addition the Flower class, the most numerous class of all (267 built), had a hull form based on a civilian whale-catcher design.

The Flower class, with only a single 4in (102mm) gun, did have good anti-submarine weapons and sensors. Disadvantages were that they were slow (at only 16 knots a surfaced U-boat could outrun them) and

were very uncomfortable for the crew in bad weather, common in the winter North Atlantic. The next most numerous type, the River class, were similar in size and performance to the Black Swans but suitable for building in civilian yards. The US Navy's Tacoma class were very similar.

US NAVY TYPES

American production of escort ships was vast. There were six classes of destroyer escorts, over 400 ships built, of similar size and capabilities to the British Hunts. The most numerous of these was the Buckley class, in

Above: The USS *England* (in early 1944) had an amazing success rate.

US Navy service from April 1943. One ship of this type, the USS *England*, achieved the unmatched feat of sinking 6 Japanese submarines within a period of 12 days in May 1944.

Other US escort vessels included a host of smaller types, usually described as submarine chasers. Many of these served with the US Coast Guard and, despite their diminutive size, they too chalked up an impressive record of over 60 submarine kills in the course of the war.

HMS *HONEYSUCKLE*

HMS *Honeysuckle* was a Flower-class corvette built on the Clyde. It is seen here during service with the Arctic convoys in 1945 in the Kola inlet alongside the escort carrier HMS *Trumpeter*. Four Flower-class ships (captured when under construction in France in 1940) were used by the Germans.

COMMISSIONED: 1940
DISPLACEMENT: 925 tons
CREW: 85
SPEED: 16 knots
ARMAMENT: 1 x 4in (102mm) i various light anti-aircraft guns; 2 x depth charge rails (as built)

Torpedo Boats and Midget Submarines

*These two varieties of warship were among the fastest and the slowest in service
with any navy, but they shared a single quality: they were the smallest
vessels capable of sinking an enemy ship of any size.*

Victims of midget submarines included several battleships and cruisers in both the Pacific and European wars. Torpedo boats also knocked out a number of cruisers and smaller warships, in addition to having numerous, probably more important, successes against transport vessels of many different kinds in all arenas of war.

TORPEDO BOATS

Varying in length from roughly 24–34m (80–110ft), the torpedo boats in service during WWII generally carried a pair of torpedo launchers and a selection of 20mm (0.79in) or similar guns and lighter weapons, and might reach top speeds of just over 40

Below: British motor torpedo boats on patrol in the Channel during the Normandy invasion.

knots. Most navies mainly used petrol engines, but the Germans in particular used diesel. The Germans were also unusual in relying on a rounded hull form, whereas most other torpedo boats followed a flat-bottomed style designed for effective planing at high speed.

German torpedo boats were in fact probably the best in service during the war. They were called *Schnellboote* ("fast boats"), but they were usually referred to on the Allied side as E-boats. Their hull shape proved very effective in poorer weather, often a problem for torpedo boats generally. Their diesel engines were also well silenced by having their exhausts underwater and were in any case less prone to catch fire after combat damage than petrol ones. A variety of types

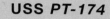

USS *PT-174*

PT-174, seen here off Rendova in January 1944, served in the Pacific from mid-1943 to the end of the war. *PT-174* was an 80ft Elco type (326 were built). These wooden boats displaced 56 tons, full load, and carried a variety of weapons in service in addition to the typical list below.

LENGTH: 24.4m (80ft)
SPEED: 41 knots
ENGINES: 3 x Packard 4m-2500; 1,500hp each
ARMAMENT: 1 x 40mm (1.58in) gun, 4 x 0.5in (12.7mm) MG; 4 x 21in (533mm) torpedoes

existed, all rather larger than most Allied designs, armed by the late war with a twin 2cm (0.79in) and a single 3.7cm (1.46in) gun, plus machine-guns and the standard pair of torpedoes.

The American equivalents (also extensively used by the British), the PT for "patrol torpedo" boats, came mainly from the Higgins and Elco companies.

The most common of several slightly different Elco boats were 24.4m (80ft) long, carried four torpedo launchers, a 20mm or 40mm (1.58in) gun and numerous machine-guns. The Higgins boats were slightly shorter and a little slower but were probably more seaworthy. Their greatest successes came not in dramatic attacks on major warships, but in numerous minor operations against Japanese supply barges and similar craft in shallow Pacific island waters where bigger Allied vessels could not go.

MIDGET SUBMARINES

Britain, Germany, Italy and Japan were the main users of midget submarines. Italy and Britain successfully used "human torpedoes" in which frogmen rode on top of a torpedo-like craft and would slowly approach an enemy anchorage to attach explosives to their targets. Britain additionally had X-craft, more like small conventional submarines, carrying massive explosive charges to drop under an anchored enemy ship. The German battleship *Tirpitz* was disabled in one such attack in Altenfjord in 1943.

Other midget submarines relied on firing torpedoes. The smallest were the German *Marder* and *Neger* types, which were in effect manned torpedoes with a second armed one slung underneath. Larger still was the *Seehund* design, a two-man vessel with two underslung torpedoes. These and several other German types appeared in small numbers and achieved scattered successes.

Japan had over 40 midget submarines in 1941, known as the *Type A* or *Ko-hyoteki*. They

Above: A Japanese midget submarine having run aground on a beach in the south-west Pacific.

were approximately 24m (80ft) long and carried two torpedoes. They were used in unsuccessful attacks on Pearl Harbor and on Sydney in Australia. However, they did damage the old British battleship *Ramillies* in a harbour in Madagascar. They were carried close to all these targets by larger "parent" submarines.

SUICIDE WEAPONS

Japan produced numerous suicide surface and submarine craft. Over 6,000 *Shinyo* motorboats were built for use against various US invasion forces. However, these small craft were ineffective – many were hunted down by PT boats. The only submarine weapon to see action was the *Kaiten*, essentially a "Long Lance" torpedo modified to be controlled by a single crewman and designed to be launched from a larger submarine. Several hundred were built but they achieved little.

Battleships and Battle-cruisers

These "capital ships", with the biggest guns and thickest armour, were traditionally seen as the decisive weapons in naval warfare. WWII saw few battleship versus battleship engagements, but these vessels still played a vital part.

The navies of the major countries fought WWII using a mix of battleships built during WWI and the 1920s and more modern vessels from the late 1930s onward.

In the inter-war period the number of battleships in service and the maximum size of new ships was limited by the Washington Naval Treaty of 1922 and other later agreements. Britain, the USA and Japan were permitted 15, 15 and 10 ships, respectively, with lower numbers for both France and Italy. Germany would also join the naval arms race, which developed as war approached, but no other navy had battleships of any significance.

Below: The USS *North Carolina* off the American coast in 1942, shortly before joining the US Pacific Fleet.

The ships surviving from the WWI era were of two types: battleships (retained by all major navies) and battle-cruisers (Britain and Japan only). Both had similar armaments and were broadly similar in size, but battle-cruisers had thinner armour in a trade-off for higher speed, a combination that had not always proved successful in WWI. Ships commissioned during WWII combined high speed and thick armour, and accordingly increased in size.

The USS *Mississippi* (New Mexico class, completed in 1917) was typical of the "WWI ships" still in service in 1939. On a displacement of 33,000 tons it carried a main armament of 12 x 14in (355mm) guns, could steam at 21 knots and was protected by side armour up to 355mm (14in) thick.

All older capital ships serving in 1939 had been modernized in the inter-war years to some degree. These changes were made principally to improve their anti-aircraft (AA) capabilities. More anti-aircraft guns were fitted, some of them new dual-purpose (DP) designs suitable for use also against surface vessels. For example, HMS *Queen Elizabeth* began the war with 20 x 4.5in (114.3mm) DP

HMS *DUKE OF YORK*

Third of the five King George V-class ships, *Duke of York*'s most notable achievement was the sinking of Germany's *Scharnhorst* in late 1943. The class's unusual main gun set-up of two quadruple turrets and a twin was troublesome at first but eventually efficient.

COMMISSIONED: 1941
DISPLACEMENT: 37,500 tons
SPEED: 30 knots
BELT ARMOUR: 15.4in (39cm) max.
ARMAMENT: 10 x 14in (355mm) + 16 x 5.24in (133mm) guns

secondary guns, compared to the 2 x 3in (76.2mm) AA guns installed when the ship entered service in 1915. Deck armour was also commonly increased to improve protection against bombs and long-range shellfire. These changes tended to increase displacement (forbidden by treaty), which was partly compensated by fitting lighter but more powerful engines.

LAST TREATY SHIPS

As war approached both Britain and the USA began building modern battleships that reflected these trends. They also attempted to keep within the treaty limitations.

The US Navy's two North Carolina and four South Dakota-class ships carried 9 x 16in (406mm) and 20 x 5in (127mm) DP guns on a displacement (as built) of 37,000 tons; the top speed was 28 knots. Britain's King George V class (the final British class to see war service) was broadly comparable, with slightly less main gun power and slightly thicker armour. America's late-war Iowa class (four ships) displaced a third more than the earlier designs and had a very high speed to escort the aircraft-carrier task forces, which by then formed the heart of the US fleet.

AXIS GIANTS

Germany's *Bismarck* and *Tirpitz*, though begun before the war, made no attempt to keep within the treaty limitations. Both ships were over 42,000 tons and were very well-protected, but

Right: The USS *Indiana* (South Dakota class) shelling the Japanese coast in 1945.

TIRPITZ

Like its sister ship *Bismarck*, *Tirpitz* achieved little for Germany. *Tirpitz* never fired its main guns against an enemy ship and was finally sunk by the RAF in 1944.

COMMISSIONED: 1941
DISPLACEMENT: 42,000 tons
SPEED: 30 knots
BELT ARMOUR: 32cm (12.6in) max.
ARMAMENT: 8 x 38cm (15in) + 12 x 15cm (5.91in) guns

had old-fashioned secondary armament featuring separate surface and AA guns.

Japan's most modern battleships were bigger yet. The 65,000-ton *Yamato* and *Musashi* (two sister ships were planned, but not built as battleships) carried 9 x 460mm (18.1in) main guns, a mass of secondary weapons and had 406mm (16in) armour. Ironically, despite their status as the most powerful battleships ever built, these two vessels were among the few WWII battleships actually to succumb to the new menace of air attack while at sea.

Aircraft Carriers

Airpower enthusiasts had been claiming since the 1920s that the aircraft carrier would soon supplant the battleship as the ultimate naval weapon. In the vast spaces of the Pacific Ocean, at least, this certainly proved to be true.

Experiments with aircraft-carrying ships were begun before WWI and the first warship to succumb to air attack was a German vessel sunk by a Japanese aircraft in 1914. But the first two true aircraft carriers with flight decks running from end to end did not enter service with Britain's Royal Navy until shortly after the end of the war.

By the time WWII began, Britain, the USA and Japan had significant aircraft-carrier forces, and built more as the war proceeded. The only other carrier in service in 1939 was France's experimental vessel *Béarn*, which did not ever see combat. Germany was building one and Italy later started two, but none of these was completed.

The three leading navies all developed ideas about carriers in the inter-war period. Both the

Below: The Independence-class light carrier USS *Langley*, with an Essex-class ship behind, at Ulithi atoll in 1944.

IJNS *KAGA*

The largest carriers in service at the start of WWII were, like *Kaga*, conversions of hulls originally planned as battleships or battle-cruisers just after WWI. A reconstruction in 1936 included the installation of an unusual downward-pointing funnel. *Kaga* participated in the Pearl Harbor attack and the raid on Darwin, but it was sunk at Midway.

COMMISSIONED: 1929
DISPLACEMENT: 38,000 tons
SPEED: 28 knots
AIRCRAFT: up to 90
GUNS: 10 x 200mm (7.87in) + 16 x 127mm (5in)

Japanese and the Americans headed in what proved to be the best direction. They realized that the carrier's best defence – and its best means of attack – were its aircraft and, therefore, the more the better.

Japan and the USA built carriers in which the hangar area under the flight deck was relatively lightly enclosed, with sides that could be opened for ventilation. This allowed the most room for aircraft.

Several of their early ships – Japan's *Akagi* and *Kaga* and the USA's *Lexington* and *Saratoga* – were particularly large, all well over 30,000 tons, and could carry up to 120 aircraft each. And with big air groups they also developed effective techniques for handling them during operations.

BRITISH DESIGNS

Britain had led the way in early carrier development but fell far behind in the inter-war years. The main reason for this was that the Royal Air Force – not the Royal Navy – controlled the supply of aircraft and pilots for maritime duties and these were given low priority. The Navy also chose to build carriers with "closed" hangar decks, which reduced aircraft capacity, although it did lead to the development of improved fire-control precautions.

In the late 1930s, aware that their obsolescent aircraft would be unable to protect the carriers completely, especially in the Mediterranean where land-based aircraft would always be within striking range, the British took this process a step further by armouring the flight decks of their new carriers. This reduced capacity even more; HMS *Illustrious*, begun in 1937, initially carried only 36 aircraft, though capacity for *Illustrious* and its 5 similar successors was increased during the war.

PACIFIC CARRIERS

Both Japan and the US Navy went to war in 1941 with a number of rather smaller carriers in addition to the largest ships already mentioned. Most were around 18,000 tons and carried 70–80 aircraft. Ships in this category included *Yorktown*, *Enterprise*, *Hiryu* and *Soryu*. Other notable vessels included the 25,000-ton *Shokaku* and *Zuikaku*, and the somewhat smaller *Wasp* and *Ranger*.

Japan introduced a number of smaller carriers in 1941–2, several being conversions of

HMS *ARK ROYAL*

Probably the most famous British ship of the early war period, HMS *Ark Royal* was wrongly reported as sunk several times by German propaganda. *Ark Royal* mainly served in the Mediterranean (including in the action off Cape Spartivento, seen below) but a Swordfish from *Ark Royal* also made the torpedo hit that crippled *Bismarck*. *Ark Royal* was finally sunk by a U-boat in November 1941.

COMMISSIONED: 1939
DISPLACEMENT: 22,000 tons
SPEED: 30 knots
AIRCRAFT: up to 60
GUNS: 16 x 4.5in (114.3mm)

other types of vessel. In all Japan completed 17 carriers (both large and small) during the war. None of these played a substantial part. This was not because they were all inadequate ships but rather that, by the time they came into service, Japan's cadre of trained naval aircrew had been wiped out and could not be quickly replaced.

The US Navy had no such problems. Its 27,000-ton Essex-class ships could carry over a hundred aircraft; 24 saw service from early 1943 onward. In addition the US Navy had the 9 ships of the Independence class of light carriers, some 10,000 tons and carrying around 40 aircraft. With ample numbers of well-trained pilots and excellent aircraft, it was these ships that led the US advance across the Pacific to defeat Japan.

Left: USS *Essex*, lead ship of its class, with about 50 of its large air group parked on deck.

Light Cruisers

Capable of giving a good account of themselves in battle, light cruisers were maids of all work, but they also were used for long-range trade protection missions, shore bombardments and other varied duties.

Cruisers carrying guns of roughly 150mm (5.91in) were probably the most ubiquitous warships of the conflict. They formed a vital part of naval task forces, both large and small, in every campaign.

WWII light cruisers can be divided into three sub-types: larger ships usually displacing at least the Washington Treaty limit of 10,000 tons or more and carrying 12 or 15 main guns, usually in triple turrets; smaller general-purpose ships of 6,000–8,000 tons, armed usually with 8 main guns in twin turrets;

Below: USS *Atlanta* (San Diego class) served in the South Pacific in 1942 but was sunk off Guadalcanal.

and anti-aircraft cruisers of 6,000 tons, armed with 10–12 smaller dual-purpose guns.

LARGE LIGHT CRUISERS
This type developed largely as a result of the pre-war arms race in the Pacific, beginning with Japan's construction of the Mogami class in the 1930s. With an impressive top speed of 35 knots, and 15 x 155mm (6.1in) guns, they supposedly had a relatively modest displacement of 8,500 tons (but, in fact, they were well over 10,000 tons).

The US Navy replied with its Brooklyn class and Britain with the Southampton class. Their wartime successors were the Cleveland (US) and Edinburgh

and Fiji (UK) classes, respectively. They were all around 10,000 tons and built with 12 x 6in (152mm) guns in triple turrets (except the Brooklyns, which had 15). During the war some ships had a 6in turret removed and replaced with smaller-calibre AA weapons.

Most of Japan's large cruisers were in the heavy-cruiser category and by Pearl Harbor, the Mogamis had also been rearmed with 203mm (7.99in) guns.

SMALL LIGHT CRUISERS
Although the US and Japanese navies had a number of cruisers of this type dating from the 1920s or earlier, including ten ships of the US Omaha class,

most vessels in this category served with European navies. This was the type of cruiser that Britain's Royal Navy most wanted to build in the inter-war period, with a good combination of long range and effective gunpower. The Leander class of the mid-1930s, for example, carried 8 x 6in guns and could make 32 knots on a displacement of some 7,200 tons. France, Germany and Italy all had comparable ships.

However, the most modern German ship, in service from 1935, was the *Nürnberg*, which

carried 9 x 15cm (5.91in) guns and was otherwise similar to the ships of the British Royal Navy.

The French and Italian Navies had slightly different priorities. In the 1930s the Italians built very fast ships (and made them seem even faster by falsifying the results of their trials) and the French replied in kind. The Italian Duca d'Aosta class (8,500 tons, 8 x 152mm/ 5.98in guns), for example, supposedly reached 37 knots.

AA Cruisers

Many of the cruisers described above had relatively limited AA capability because their main gun mountings and control systems were only suitable for use against surface targets. As the war progressed, ships in all navies gained additional light AA guns, but Britain and the USA also saw a need for cruisers with greatly enhanced heavy AA firepower. The US Navy's San Diego and Britain's Dido and Bellona classes all carried large batteries of dual-purpose main guns, 10 x 5.25in (133mm) for the Didos and 12 or even 16 x 5in (127mm) for the San Diegos. All were also fast ships, capable of 33 or 34 knots to keep up with fast aircraft carrier forces.

Above: The *Giuseppe Garibaldi* carried 10 x 152mm (5.98in) guns and could reach a reported 34 knots.

KÖLN

The German Navy built three K-class cruisers in the late 1920s. Unusually, six of the nine main guns were aft. In service *Köln* and its sisters were found to lack stability in heavy weather. In 1940 *Köln* participated in the invasion of Norway but saw little action thereafter before being sunk by air attack in port in 1945.

COMMISSIONED: 1930
DISPLACEMENT: 6,700 tons
SPEED: 32 knots
AIRCRAFT: 2 x Arado 196
ARMAMENT: 9 x 15cm (5.9in) + 6 x 8.8cm (3.46in) guns; 12 x 533mm (21in) torpedo tubes

HMS AJAX

One of the five British Leander-class light cruisers, *Ajax* had an eventful war career. In 1939 *Ajax* joined two other cruisers, *Exeter* and *Achilles*, in hunting down the *Graf Spee*. In 1944 *Ajax* was one of the ships in the D-Day bombardment force. This record in action proved the usefulness of the relatively small cruisers of this type.

COMMISSIONED: 1935
DISPLACEMENT: 7,200 tons
SPEED: 32 knots
ARMOUR: 102mm (4in) max.
ARMAMENT: 8 x 6in (152mm) + 8 x 4in (102mm) guns; 8 x 21in (533mm) torpedo tubes

Escort Carriers

No escort carriers existed in 1939, but by the end of the war Britain and the USA had well over a hundred ships of this type protecting the vital Atlantic supply routes and supporting amphibious operations in the Pacific.

One of the simplest lessons of WWII was that air power was vital in every area of warfare, by sea as much as by land. The USA, Britain and Japan were the only countries to operate large "fleet carriers" with their main naval forces and were also the only countries to deploy smaller "escort carriers" for what were sometimes seen as more mundane, second-line duties (though Japan's half dozen such completed vessels achieved nothing).

Convoy Air Cover

As the Battle of the Atlantic developed in intensity from the summer of 1940, the British authorities soon decided their Atlantic convoys needed air protection. Since fleet carriers were too scarce and valuable for use in this role, different ships and techniques were devised. At that point the main task envisaged for such ships was to counter the German Focke-Wulf Kondor aircraft, which were attacking convoys and homing-in U-boat packs.

The first expedient, from April 1941, was to fit a single aircraft-launching catapult to a merchant ship to carry a fighter. There were four Royal Navy fighter catapult ships and 35 merchant navy catapult aircraft merchant (CAM) ships. After his mission the pilot either had to make for land or ditch his plane near the convoy and hope to be picked up. Remarkably, this perilous process sometimes worked; six German aircraft are said to have been shot down by CAM-ship aircraft, though a number of the ships were themselves sunk by U-boats.

The first true escort carrier was HMS *Audacity*, operational in June 1941. *Audacity* only sailed with three convoys before being sunk by a U-boat in December 1941, but it had already clearly proved its worth.

By then the US Navy had taken delivery of its first escort carrier and was building more,

Below: HMS *Audacity*, a converted merchant ship, carried only eight fighters for convoy air defence.

both for its own use and for the Royal Navy. In all some 130 escort carriers were built, or converted from existing merchant-ship or auxiliary-cruiser hulls.

The Bogue and Casablanca classes were the main types. They usually operated 20–35 aircraft, often a mix of about one-third fighters and two-thirds bomber/reconnaissance

Right: The CAM-ship *Empire Spray* with a Sea Hurricane fighter on its catapult, seen in October 1941.

types. They were much slower than fleet carriers and only lightly built, but it was never intended that they should operate in areas where air or surface attack was a significant risk.

For a variety of reasons, few escort carriers came into service on the Atlantic convoy routes until 1943. However, from then until the end of the war, they protected many convoys and hunted down and sank numerous U-boats. In June 1944 the escort carrier USS *Guadalcanal* even assisted in the capture of a German submarine, U-505.

From mid-1943 there were also 19 British merchant aircraft carriers (MAC ships), merchant ships given a very basic flight deck and three or four Swordfish aircraft equipped for the antisubmarine role. These also carried normal cargoes and sailed with convoys; no convoy that included a MAC ship ever lost a vessel to U-boat attack.

PACIFIC COMBATS

Some escort carriers were used to train carrier aircrews, but many also saw extensive combat service in the Pacific. As the US counter-offensive developed, escort carrier groups were used to provide close support to the various landing forces, while the main fleet carrier groups wore down Japanese air power and guarded against interventions by the Japanese fleet.

Right: The USS *Makin Island*, a Casablanca-class ship, seen near Leyte in November 1944 early in its combat career.

At least that was the theory. At Leyte Gulf, however, it went drastically wrong. In a remarkable action the escort carrier groups successfully fought off an attack by some of the Japanese Navy's most powerful ships. One escort carrier was sunk by gunfire in this action and another by a kamikaze aircraft.

Naval Weapons and Electronics

No entirely new naval weapons were introduced in the course of WWII, but the existing armoury of guns, torpedoes and depth charges was given new accuracy and striking power by developments in control systems and detection equipment.

Guns in service at sea in WWII ranged from the 460mm (18.1in) monsters fitted to Japan's *Yamato* and its sister ships to the light anti-aircraft weapons of 20mm (0.79in) and upward, which were carried by almost every fighting vessel of all countries' navies.

As well as firing truly formidable projectiles (1,460kg/3,220lb for the *Yamato*), the big guns had a very considerable reach. The longest-range hit ever made by a gun on a moving target – 24km (15 miles) – was by a 15in (380mm) on HMS *Warspite* against the Italian *Giulio Cesare* in July 1940.

Below: The carrier USS *Cowpens* in 1943. SC, SG and SK radar aerials are among the equipment on view, illustrating radar's importance.

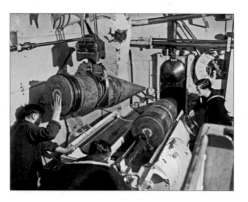

Above: Handling 929kg (2,048lb) 16in (406mm) shells in the magazine of the battleship HMS *Nelson*.

TORPEDOES

The guns used by all navies were generally comparable in performance (though poorly manufactured Italian shells were notably inaccurate). However, this was less true with the other major anti-ship weapon – the torpedo.

There were two main torpedo propulsion systems. The more common used compressed gas and oil or alcohol fuel to drive the torpedo engine. This gave the best speed/range combination but left a wake in the water behind the torpedo, which could give the target sufficient warning to dodge. The best such torpedo was the 610mm (24in) Japanese Type 93, usually known by the nickname of "Long Lance". This torpedo used compressed oxygen, rather than air, to achieve a far better performance than any other type.

Germany, and later the US Navy, also used battery-powered torpedoes. These had shorter ranges but left no wake.

Early-war torpedoes were designed to run at a fixed depth in a straight line and to detonate either by contact or underneath an enemy ship, by using a magnetic influence device. Both the Germans and Americans had numerous problems with unreliable depth-keeping for many months after they joined the war and all nations found their magnetic influence warheads rather temperamental.

Developments during the war included German torpedoes that could follow a zigzag or looping course to increase the chances of a hit, and acoustic homing torpedoes, produced by both the Germans and the Allies, used against submerged submarines or other targets.

Above: The *Graf Spee* in December 1939, showing signs of damage after the Battle of the River Plate. The ship's Seetakt radar aerial can be seen at the top of the picture.

The main anti-submarine weapons were unguided underwater bombs known as depth charges. These simply sank through the water to explode at a pre-set depth. Typically they had to detonate within 10m (33ft) of a submarine to sink it, so several were usually dropped in a "pattern" with slightly different settings. Depth charges were improved during the war by being filled with increasingly powerful explosive compounds.

Depth charges were supplemented by smaller weapons, either contact or depth fused, which could be thrown ahead of the attacking ship. The most successful were the British Hedgehog and Squid types.

ELECTRONICS

The main underwater sensor in use was sonar (officially called asdic in the Royal Navy until 1943). This used sound pulses to find the range and bearing of a target but did not determine the depth of the submarine; it was also blind in the area underneath the ship (hence the utility of forward-firing weapons).

Radar naturally played an important part in the war at sea, detecting enemy ships and aircraft and giving gunnery ranges in bad weather and at night. Germany's Seetakt type, in service in 1939, was a highly effective early-war design. Later-war Allied designs, like the British Type 271 and others, could detect a target as small as a submarine periscope.

Above: A depth charge being deployed from a US escort.

Just as important as target detection and ranging systems was equipment to translate this and other information into firing data. The US Navy in particular developed effective anti-aircraft control systems and the American torpedo data computer fitted in submarines was superior to its equivalents in use in other navies.

Below: A 20mm (0.79in) anti-aircraft gun position on the foredeck of the battleship USS *Iowa* in 1943. Two of the ship's 16in (406mm) main gun turrets can be seen behind.

Naval Fighters

Like their land-based counterparts, fighters designed for operations from aircraft carriers had to be fast, manoeuvrable and well armed, but long range and robust construction for operations in difficult maritime conditions were equally valuable.

Since only Britain, the USA and Japan operated aircraft carriers, these were the only nations that had aircraft in this class, though on occasion the aircraft concerned also operated from land bases.

BRITISH DESIGNS

Britain's early-war naval fighters were particularly poor. In 1939 Britain's Fleet Air Arm still employed the biplane Sea

Below: Grumman Hellcats leading an air group preparing to take off from the carrier *Lexington* in 1944.

Gladiator type and also had the turret-armed Blackburn Roc, which (though a monoplane) was even slower than the Gladiator. These were replaced from 1940 by the Fairey Fulmar, which fought reasonably effectively against Italian aircraft in the Mediterranean but did not compare well with other nations' designs. The later Fairey Firefly, also a relatively large two-seat aircraft, had performance of a more modern standard, with a top speed of 508kph (316mph), and could also carry a useful bomb load.

The best home-made pure fighters employed afloat by the Royal Navy were conversions of the Spitfire, known in naval service as the Seafire. Various marks of Seafire were used and, like the parent design, were fast, manoeuvrable and well armed – but lacking in range. In the later-war years most naval fighters in British service were the US types described below.

THE JAPANESE NAVY

The best-known Japanese naval fighters came from the Mitsubishi company. The A5M

Above: A formation of US Navy Grumman F4F Wildcats in flight.

Above: Like other two-seat fighters, the Fairey Fulmar did not fare well in combat with modern single-seat designs, despite its heavy armament.

"Claude" served in China in the late 1930s and to some extent in the early part of the Pacific War. With a top speed of some 435kph (270mph), it was surprisingly fast for a fixed-undercarriage design and highly manoeuvrable.

The next Mitsubishi fighter – the A6M Type 0 "Zeke" (or "Zero") – was truly remarkable. In service from 1940, it had unequalled combat manoeuvrability at that time, was well armed with 2 x 20mm (0.79in) cannon and 2 machine-guns and had an astonishing 950km (600 mile) radius of action. It outclassed all Allied opponents until at least late 1942. The more powerful late-war A6M5 variant was the most-produced Zero. However, by then the Allies had well-trained pilots in abundance and aircraft with the heavy armament and performance to exploit the Zero's weaknesses of light construction and lack of armour for the pilot.

Other notable Japanese Navy fighters were various models of the Mitsubishi J2M Raiden "Jack" and the Kawanishi N1K Shiden "George". These mostly served in land-based roles, latterly in defence of the Home Islands against American B-29 bombing raids.

AMERICAN TYPES

The US Navy also began the war with a soon-to-be-phased-out pre-war design, the Brewster F2A Buffalo, the US Navy's first monoplane fighter. This served at Midway and with the British RAF in Malaya in 1941–2 but was clearly no match for the Zero.

Already replacing it by then was the Grumman F4F Wildcat (also known as the Martlet in British service). Updated variants of the Wildcat remained in service until 1945. By then it had been supplemented by a larger and more powerful Grumman design – the F6F Hellcat – which some commentators describe as the best carrier fighter of the war. It was highly manoeuvrable and extremely robust, an advantage not just in combat but also in the common occurrence of heavy carrier landings. With a top speed of 620kph (385mph), it had more than adequate performance.

Challenging the Hellcat was the US Navy's other main late-war fighter – the Chance Vought

---

MITSUBISHI A6M2 ZERO

In 1941–2 the Zero fighter seemed invincible, with better performance than any Allied aircraft. However, it was very lightly built with at first no cockpit armour or self-sealing fuel tanks. These were introduced in later models in use until 1945.

CREW: 1
SPEED: 533kph (331mph)
RANGE: 3,100km (1,930 miles) with drop tank
ENGINE: 940hp Nakajima NK1C Sakae radial
ARMAMENT: 2 x 20mm (0.79in) cannon + 2 x 7.7mm (0.303in) machine-guns

---

F4U Corsair (in service from October 1942). Significantly faster than the Hellcat – over 700kph (435mph) in late-war variants – the F4U was also used effectively as a fighter-bomber.

Submarine Classes

WWII submarines had limited capabilities, but no one doubted that they were potentially war-winning weapons. Germany's 1,000 U-boats failed in the Battle of the Atlantic, but the US Navy's submarines fatally weakened Japan.

Germany's U-boat force depended for most of the war on two main designs: the smaller (750 tons surfaced) Type VII and larger (1,000 tons) Type IX. These designs, clearly derived from WWI U-boats, were both well-engineered and robustly built for deep diving.

U-BOAT DEVELOPMENTS

Ten Type XIV supply U-boats were also built. These played an important role in extending the operational range, especially of the Type VIIs, but all the Type XIVs were hunted down as a priority by the Allied forces using code-breaking information. By the mid-war years the U-boats were outmatched by

Below: The Italian Tritone-class boat *Marea* off Bermuda in 1944. *Marea* was then being used by the Allies for anti-submarine training.

Allied anti-submarine forces, so work on new technologies to overcome this was stepped up. First introduced was a breathing tube, or *Schnorchel* (a pre-war Dutch invention), designed to enable the submarine to run its main engines while submerged and difficult to detect. This worked up to a point but had various disadvantages when in use. More promising was work to streamline submarine hulls

Above: The Gato-class USS *Barb*, seen in San Francisco Bay in May 1945, returning to action after a refit.

and step up battery capacity. A few Type XXI and XXIII U-boats using this technology came into service shortly before the end of the war – their high underwater speed made them very difficult to counter. More might have been built if Germany had not wasted much

effort on the abortive development of the Walther system, which used hydrogen peroxide to provide oxygen so that the main engines could run when the boat was submerged.

EUROPEAN CLASSES

Britain had three main classes of submarine during the war: U, S and T (in ascending order of size). The 550-ton U-class boats were designed for training duties but, in the event, were used effectively in action in the confined Mediterranean waters. All the British boats had the merit of being fast-diving and carrying a heavy armament of bow torpedo tubes – eight in the T class compared to six or even four in other nations' boats.

Submarines built for Pacific service (including the British T class) tended to be larger than those designed for European waters. In 1939 the largest submarine in service was France's *Surcouf* – 3,250 tons, armed with a twin 203mm (7.99in) turret and carrying a floatplane.

JAPANESE SUBMARINES

Japan's wartime I-400 class (three built) were even bigger, at 5,200 tons, and could carry three aircraft, intended to attack the locks on the Panama Canal. Other nations experimented with monster submarines before WWII, but these were the only examples to see any service.

Japan's standard submarines were unremarkable: relatively slow-diving and unable to dive very deep. Their advantage was using a 533mm (21in) version of the famous "Long Lance" torpedo, by far the best submarine torpedo of the war. Japanese tactics also emphasized attacks on

HMS *TUDOR*

The British T-class submarine *Tudor* was commissioned in 1944 and served against Japan to the end of the war, sinking ten ships. In all, 53 boats of the T class were completed, several of them serving with the Dutch Navy.

DISPLACEMENT: 1,290 tons surfaced; 1,560 tons submerged
LENGTH: 84.3m (276.5ft)
SURFACE SPEED: 15.5 knots
SUBMERGED SPEED: 9 knots
ARMAMENT: 11 x 21in (533mm) torpedo tubes + 1 x 4in (102mm) gun

enemy warships and disregarded attacks on supply ships. Though Japanese submarines sank the carriers *Wasp* and *Yorktown* among other successes, their contribution was limited. The largest-sized class was the 2,200-ton I-15 type.

US NAVY TYPES

American fleet submarines were all of high quality. The similar Gato, Balao and Tench classes saw much service. They were all roughly 1,500 tons and well designed, both in terms of radar and sonar equipment, as well as incidentals like air conditioning that helped make long Pacific patrols more comfortable for the crews. Unfortunately, for more than a year after Pearl Harbor, their torpedoes were very poor. When this fault was rectified US submarines practically wiped out the Japanese merchant fleet and sank many of the naval vessels sent to hunt them down.

Below: A U-boat after its surrender in 1945. Note the heavy anti-aircraft armament carried by most U-boats by this time.

Destroyers

Destroyers were multi-purpose warships, fast and deadly hunters of surface ships and submarines with their torpedo and depth-charge armament. They served in their hundreds and saw combat after combat in every theatre of war.

Destroyers were invented to protect battlefleets from torpedo attack, and to carry out such attacks themselves. These essentially remained their main functions in WWII, though by then of course torpedo attack could come from submarines as well as surface craft.

Destroyers of WWII were generally 1,500–2,000 tons displacement and typically carried 4–6 main guns of 127mm (5in) or similar calibre and 8–10 torpedo tubes (TT), and had a top speed of about 35 knots. All also carried depth-charge equipment and a number of lighter anti-aircraft guns. More of both these types of weapon generally were added as the war progressed, along with new and improved varieties of radar and sonar equipment. Britain, the USA and Japan each began the war with over 100 destroyers in

service, built many more in the course of the conflict – and each lost more than 100 in combat.

EUROPEAN DESIGNS

Among European navies Britain built relatively small destroyers in the inter-war years. Known as the A to I classes (a class of nine or so was built yearly during the 1930s), these 1,400-ton ships carried 4 x 4.7in (119mm) guns and 8 or 10 TT. However, the 4.7in gun could not be used for AA defence, so these ships were poorly equipped to withstand air attack. Britain also had the larger Tribal class with 8 x 4.7in guns and a reduced torpedo armament. Both France and Italy built some extremely large destroyers, including the Fantasque and Navigatori classes; these were large and very fast ships but paid a price in seaworthiness and reliability.

HMAS *NESTOR*

Built in Britain and commissioned in 1941, the *Nestor* served in the *Bismarck* chase and was sunk during a Malta convoy operation in June 1942. *Nestor* was one of 24 similar J, K and N class ships built for the British and Allied navies, 1937–42. Although an Australian Navy ship, *Nestor* never visited Australia.

DISPLACEMENT: 1,770 tons standard, 2,300 tons full load
CREW: 180
SPEED: 36 knots
RANGE: 5,500nm (10,200km) at 15 knots (27.8kph)
LENGTH: 111.4m (356.5ft)
BEAM: 10.9m (35.75ft)
ARMAMENT: 6 x 4.7in (119mm) guns + 5 x 21in (533 mm) TT; 1 x 4in (102mm) AA gun + numerous light AA weapons

Left: The Kagero-class *Yukikaze*, pictured in January 1940. *Yukikaze* was the only one of the 19 ships in the class to survive the war.

Above: USS *Fletcher* in July 1942. The 177-ship Fletcher class was the most numerous destroyer type ever.

Germany's pre-war and wartime ships were a mix of larger vessels classed as "destroyers" and smaller "torpedo boats". Destroyer or *Zerstörer* types were typically 2,400 tons, with 5 x 12.7cm (5in) guns. British wartime destroyers, in lettered classes up to W, were generally slightly larger than their predecessors, with better AA capability. Some had 4in (102mm) AA guns as main armament instead of the 4.7in weapons.

PACIFIC NAVIES

Japan and the USA favoured slightly larger ships than the British for their pre-war classes and had the advantage of having suitable dual-purpose (DP) surface/AA gun mounts with which to arm them. Japan also had the 610mm (24in) "Long Lance" torpedo, far superior to anything in Allied service. In addition the Japanese fitted their ships with torpedo reloading equipment that could be used in action, allowing multiple attacks to be carried out.

Right: The USS *Wilson*, one of ten Benham-class destroyers of the US Navy, seen in January 1941.

Japan's Fubuki class (24 completed by 1932) were the most powerful destroyers in the world when built (1,800 tons, 6 x 127mm, 9 TT); they proved too flimsy so were extensively rebuilt early in their service. Another notable class was the 2,000-ton Kagero type with similar armament to the Fubukis.

The US Navy had the best DP main gun: the 5in/38-calibre Mark 12, fitted in most US destroyers from the Farragut class (1934, 1,400 tons, 5 x 5in, 8 TT) onward. The Porter class of 1936–7 was larger (1,850 tons, 8 x 5in), in an attempt to match the big Japanese designs, but these destroyers had stability and seaworthiness problems.

Above: The German destroyer *Z14* or *Friedrich Ihn* pictured in 1942, one of 12 ships of the 1934A class.

However, US Navy classes built during the war years were the best destroyers of the time. The Fletcher class (2,100 tons, 5 x 5in, 10 TT, 35 knots) had an excellent balance of firepower, stability and speed, and the capacity to fit additional AA guns and other equipment shown to be necessary by wartime experience. The later Allen M. Sumner and Gearing classes were slightly bigger but generally similar, with the exception that the Fletchers' five single 5in mounts were replaced by three twin turrets.

Index